Presented To

_____

Presented By

_____

Date

You are my sheep, the
sheep of my pasture
and I am your God,
says the Lord GOD.

Ezekiel 34:31 NRSV

Jesus Speaks To Women

Blessed are the
pure in heart, for
they shall see God.

Matthew 5:8 NASB

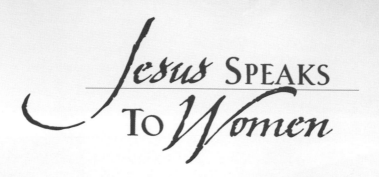

Jesus Speaks To Women

MEDITATIONS
ON THE
WORDS OF JESUS

BETHANYHOUSE

Minneapolis, Minnesota

Jesus Speaks to Women

Copyright © 2004 by GRQ, Inc.
Brentwood, Tennessee 37027

Published by Bethany House Publishers
11400 Hampshire Avenue South
Bloomington, Minnesota 55438
www.bethanyhouse.com

Bethany House Publishers is a Division of Baker Book House Company, Grand Rapids, Michigan.

Scripture quotations noted CEV are taken from THE CONTEMPORARY ENGLISH VERSION. © 1991 by the American Bible Society. Used by permission.

Scripture quotations noted GOD'S WORD are taken from *God's Word*. *God's Word* is a copyrighted work of God's Word to the Nations Bible Society. Quotations are used by permission. Copyright 1995 by God's Word to the Nations Bible Society. All rights reserved.

Scripture quotations noted GNT are taken from GOOD NEWS TRANSLATION, SECOND EDITION, Copyright © 1992 by the American Bible Society. Used by permission. All rights reserved.

Scripture quotations noted KJV are taken from the King James Version of the Holy Bible.

Scripture quotations noted THE MESSAGE are taken from *THE MESSAGE: The New Testament, Psalms and Proverbs*. Copyright © 1993, 1994, 1995 by Eugene H. Peterson. All rights reserved.

Scripture quotations noted NASB are taken from the NEW AMERICAN STANDARD BIBLE® Copyright © 1960, 1962, 1963–1968, 1971, 1973–1975, 1977, 1995 by the Lockman Foundation. Used by permission.

Scripture quotations noted NCV are taken from The Holy Bible, New Century Version, copyright © 1987, 1988, 1991 by Word Publishing, Dallas, Texas.

Scripture quotations noted NIV are taken from the *Holy Bible: New International Version* (North American Edition)®. Copyright © 1973–1978, 1984, by the International Bible Society. Used by permission of Zondervan. All rights reserved.

Scripture quotations noted NIrV are taken from the HOLY BIBLE, NEW INTERNATIONAL READER'S VERSION™, Copyright © 1995, 1996, 1998 by the International Bible Society. Used by permission of The Zondervan Corporation. All rights reserved.

Scripture quotations noted NKJV are taken from THE NEW KING JAMES VERSION. Copyright © 1979, 1980, 1982, Thomas Nelson, Inc., Publishers.

Scripture quotation noted NLT are taken from the *Holy Bible*, New Living Translation, copyright © 1996. Used by permission of Tyndale House Publishers, Inc., Wheaton, Illinois 60189. All rights reserved.

Scripture quotations noted NRSV are taken from the New Revised Standard Version of the Bible, copyright © 1989 by the Division of Christian Education of the National Council of the Churches of Christ in the USA. Used by permission. All rights reserved.

Library of Congress Control Number 2004010923
ISBN 0-7642-2916-8

Editor: Lila Empson
Manuscript written and compiled by Rebecca Currington in cooperation
    with Snapdragon Editorial Group, Inc.
Design: Garborg and Associates

04 05 06   4 3 2 1

Walk in love, as Christ
also has loved us and
given Himself for us.

Ephesians 5:2 NKJV

Contents

Introduction 10

1. The Art of Asking (*Persistence*) 12

2. Let Your Light Shine (*Good Deeds*) 16

3. Great Love (*Forgiveness*) 20

4. A Drink of Living Water (*Eternal Life*) 24

5. Full and Overflowing (*Obedience*) 28

6. A Better Way (*Enemies*) 32

7. United in Purpose (*God's Will*) 36

8. A Good Measure (*Judgment*) 40

9. From the Heart (*Purity*) 44

10. Giving in Secret (*Benevolence*) 48

11. A Solitary Place (*Rest*) 52

12. Say the Word (*Faith*) 56

13. Spirit and Truth (*Worship*) 60

14. Treasure in Heaven (*Materialism*) 64

15. Nothing to Eat (*Compassion*) 68

16. Well Done (*Faithfulness*) 72

17. Set Free (*Truth*) 76

18. Step Out of the Boat (*Courage*) 80

19. Follow Me (*Commitment*) 84

20. The Good Shepherd (*God's Care*) 88

21. The King Is Coming (*Watchfulness*) 92

22. A Sound Mind (*Restoration*) 96

23. This Very Night (*Betrayal*) 100

24. The Greatest (*Selflessness*) 104

25. A House Divided (*Unity*) 108

26. For My Sake (*Expectations*) 112

27. More Than Food (*God's Kingdom*) 116

28. Lip Service (*Honoring God*) 120

29. The Righteous Judge (*Justice*) 124

30. Watch and Pray (*Perseverance*) 128

31. Born Again (*Revelation*) 132

32. Don't Be Fooled (*Discernment*) 136

33. One Flesh (*Marriage*) 140

34. Not As the World Gives (*Peace*) 144

35. A Place for You (*Comfort*) 148

36. All These Things (*Priorities*) 152

37. The Servant of All (*Service*) 156

38. Rejoicing Hearts (*Joy*) 160

39. Filled With God (*Righteousness*) 164

40. The Greatest Commandment (*Love*) 168

41. Rejoice and Be Glad (*Persecution*) 172

42. Receiving the Kingdom (*Greed*) 176

43. The Cost of Commitment (*Sacrifice*) 180

44. What Was Promised (*Power*) 184

45. In Jesus' Name (*Authority*) 188

Introduction

Let the Word of Christ—the Message—have the run of the house. Give it plenty of room in your lives.

Colossians 3:16 THE MESSAGE

Jesus' words aren't like anyone else's. They are alive and powerful, infused with divinity. And they are timeless—just as relevant today as they were when Jesus spoke them on the grassy slopes of the Mount of Olives, along the shores of the Sea of Galilee, in the quiet stillness of the Garden of Gethsemane, outside the stone walls of the Temple, in the cloistered privacy of a borrowed upstairs room.

Before you read the first page of *Jesus Speaks to Women*, make a conscious decision to let Jesus' words penetrate your heart and mind. Determine to take them into your home, into your workplace, into your life— embrace them, and let them make you the woman of faith and power that God intends for you to be.

The Art of Asking

Jesus said, "Ask, and it will be given you; search, and you will find; knock, and the door will be opened for you."

Luke 11:9 NRSV

The Story Behind What Jesus Said

When Jesus' disciples asked him to teach them about prayer, he told the story of a man who knocked on the door of a friend in the middle of the night asking to borrow three loaves of bread. His friend responded, "Go away. We're all in bed for the night. I can't help you!"

But the man persisted. "Please, friend, I need that bread. I have unexpected company who have traveled a long way. They're hungry, and I have nothing to feed them. Come on, friend, can't you help me out?"

Exasperated, the man's friend decided he could no longer bear the persistent knocking and pleading. He got out of bed, went to the door, and handed over the loaves of bread.

Reflections on the Words of Jesus

Have you been praying about a particular need in your life? Maybe you've been asking for a long time but the answer hasn't yet become evident. Don't give up. Keep praying. And keep your eyes focused not on the object of your prayer but on the one to whom you are addressing your request.

The man in the story persisted not because he had faith that the bread would appear if he kept asking for it, but because he had faith in his friend. He didn't move on to the next house. He kept knocking on the door of the man he knew would help him.

Place your confidence in God—in his mercy, compassion, faithfulness, and wisdom. He hears and answers every prayer, although it may not be in the manner you expect. Keep knocking until his perfect answer comes at his perfect time.

One Final Thought

God's answer, God's provision, and God's guidance are worth waiting for. Place your confidence in him, keep praying, and don't give up.

Timeless Wisdom for Everyday Living

Everyone who asks, receives. Everyone who seeks, finds. And the door is opened to everyone who knocks. Matthew 7:8 NLT

If you believe, you will receive whatever you ask for in prayer.
Matthew 21:22 GNT

When you search for me, you will find me; if you seek me with all your heart.
Jeremiah 29:13 NRSV

Jesus told them a parable about their need to pray always and not to lose heart.
Luke 18:1 NRSV

We can be confident that [God] will listen to us whenever we ask him for anything in line with his will.
1 John 5:14 NLT

If you make yourselves at home with me [Jesus] and my words are at home in you, you can be sure that whatever you ask will be listened to and acted upon. John 15:7 THE MESSAGE

Storm the throne of grace and persevere therein, and mercy will come down.

John Wesley

The secret of the constancy of grace and virtue lies in the perseverance in prayer.

John Cassian

The value of consistent prayer is not that He will hear us, but that we will hear Him.

William McGill

To pray effectively we must want what God wants—that and that only is to pray in the will of God.

A. W. Tozer

Pray, always pray; when sickness wastes thy frame, prayer brings the healing power of Jesus' name.   A. B. Simpson

It is because God has promised certain things that we can ask for them with the full assurance of faith.

A. W. Pink

He who seeks the Father more than anything he can give is likely to have what he asks, for he is not likely to ask amiss.

George Macdonald

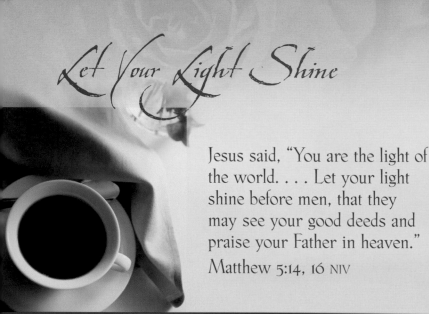

Let Your Light Shine

Jesus said, "You are the light of the world. . . . Let your light shine before men, that they may see your good deeds and praise your Father in heaven."
Matthew 5:14, 16 NIV

The Story Behind What Jesus Said

Several women sat together on the grass listening intently—so intently that they were unaware of the heat of the day or those seated around them. Their attention was focused on one man, a teacher—nondescript in appearance but authoritative in speech.

The women had been following the teacher for days. They joined the crowds because they had been told that a great prophet was performing miracles. But soon their curiosity turned to awe as the amazing teacher talked not about power and conquest, but an inner kingdom that exists in the hearts of those who love God.

That kingdom, the teacher said, would be evident in their good deeds—true acts of kindness that would illuminate the world around them.

Reflections on the Words of Jesus

As a woman, you are in a unique position to bring glory to God through the good deeds you do. Your instinct to nurture and encourage is God given and can reach far beyond your inner circle of family and friends.

Your good deeds can take many forms. They might be as simple as a word, a hug, or a smile, or as exacting as sitting beside the bedside of someone in the throes of a long, painful illness. What makes any deed good is that it is taken from the good treasure of the kingdom in your heart and that it brings praise to God.

Jesus no longer teaches from the Galilean hillsides. He no longer reaches out his hand to touch the hurting—except through you. You are his hands, his feet, his voice on earth. Let your actions reflect the light of God shining from his mighty kingdom inside you.

One Final Thought

Jesus' good deeds identified him as the Light of the World. Your good deeds reflect that same Light into your world.

Timeless Wisdom for Everyday Living

I the LORD test the mind and search the heart, to give to all according to their ways, according to the fruit of their doings. Jeremiah 17:10 NRSV

As the body without the spirit is dead, so faith without deeds is dead.

James 2:26 NIV

Good deeds are obvious, and even those that are not cannot be hidden.

1 Timothy 5:25 NIV

God has made us what we are, and in our union with Christ Jesus he has created us for a life of good deeds, which he has already prepared for us to do.

Ephesians 2:10 GNT

Are there any of you who are wise and understanding? You are to prove it by your good life, by your good deeds performed with humility and wisdom.

James 3:13 GNT

Let us consider how we may spur one another on toward love and good deeds. Hebrews 10:24 NIV

Goodness is something so simple: always live for others, never to seek one's own advantage.

Dag Hammarskjöld

An act of goodness, the least act of true goodness, is indeed the best proof of the existence of God.

Jacques Maritain

How far that little candle throws his beams! So shines a good deed in a naughty world.

William Shakespeare

Our Lord does not care so much for the importance of our works as for the love with which they are done.

Saint Teresa of Avila

We are not saved by good works, but for good works. Author Unknown

The value of good works is not based on their number and excellence, but on the love of God which prompts him to do these things.

Saint John of the Cross

Measure your day, not by what you harvest, but by what you plant.

Author Unknown

Great Love

Jesus said, "Look at this woman kneeling here. . . . Her sins—and they are many—have been forgiven, so she has shown me much love."

Luke 7:44, 47 NLT

The Story Behind What Jesus Said

Jesus was dining one day at the home of one of the city's most prominent religious leaders, a Pharisee named Simon, when suddenly a woman appeared in the room. Head down and eyes averted, she dropped to her knees at his feet. Weeping quietly, her tears fell on Jesus' feet and she wiped them away with her hair. Then she kissed his feet and poured perfume on them.

Jesus' host was appalled by the woman's behavior—and Jesus' relaxed response to her actions. Simon had invited Jesus into his home because he felt the popular teacher might be a prophet. Now he wasn't so sure. Wouldn't a prophet recognize that this woman lived a sinful life? Wouldn't he brush aside her touch?

Reflections on the Words of Jesus

Simon the Pharisee saw a tragic figure kneeling there on the floor at Jesus' feet. But Jesus saw someone else—a woman transformed by forgiveness. Simon saw a sinner, a castoff, a person who was too unclean to touch. But Jesus saw an entirely new creation. Simon saw tears of grief and regret. But Jesus saw tears of hope and thankfulness and love.

It's difficult for human beings to comprehend the creative power of God's forgiveness. Humans tend to think in terms of patching over or covering up. But when God forgives, he re-creates.

Have you experienced the power of God's forgiveness? If so, you understand what motivated the weeping woman and what provoked her great love for Jesus. You know the joy of being able to put your mistakes behind you and begin again. You've received a precious gift. Cherish the one who gave it to you.

One Final Thought

Receiving God's forgiveness, priceless but freely given, evokes great love and devotion in you and in everyone who has received it.

If we confess our sins to God, he will keep his promise and do what is right: he will forgive us our sins and purify us from all our wrongdoing.

1 John 1:9 GNT

If you forgive others their trespasses, your heavenly Father will also forgive you.

Matthew 6:14 NRSV

There is now no condemnation for those who are in Christ Jesus, because through Christ Jesus the law of the Spirit of life set me free from the law of sin and death.

Romans 8:1–2 NIV

As far as the east is from the west, so far he removes our transgressions from us.

Psalm 103:12 NRSV

Peter said to them, "Each one of you must turn away from your sins and be baptized in the name of Jesus Christ, so that your sins will be forgiven; and you will receive God's gift, the Holy Spirit."

Acts 2:38 GNT

Happy are those whose transgression is forgiven, whose sin is covered.   Psalm 32:1 NRSV

Nothing in this world bears the impress of the Son of God so surely as forgiveness.

Alice Cary

Forgiveness is man's deepest need and highest achievement.

Horace Bushnell

When Christ's hands were nailed to the cross, he also nailed your sins to the cross.

Saint Bernard of Clairvaux

Forgetting with God is a divine attribute; God's forgiveness forgets.

Oswald Chambers

It is idle for us to say that we know that God has forgiven us if we are not loving and forgiving ourselves. Martyn Lloyd-Jones

In these days of guilt complexes, perhaps the most glorious word in the English language is "forgiveness."

Billy Graham

The most marvelous ingredient in the forgiveness of God is that he also forgets, the one thing a human being can never do. Forgiving with God is a divine attribute; God's forgiveness forgets.

Oswald Chambers

A Drink of Living Water

Jesus said, "Those who drink of the water that I will give them will never be thirsty. The water that I will give will become in them a spring of water gushing up to eternal life." John 4:14 NRSV

The Story Behind What Jesus Said

It was not the most comfortable time of day to walk to the village well for water. However, the hot noonday sun shielded the woman from the prying eyes and gossiping tongues that were present in the cool of the morning. The woman knew her promiscuous lifestyle had made her an outcast—but even outcasts get thirsty.

A stranger sat nearby. A Jew. When he asked for a drink of water, she didn't know what to think. Jews despised the Samaritans, and men were not supposed to speak to unescorted women. However, the man did more than ask for a favor. He offered her a drink of living water in return—this water, he told her, would permanently quench her thirst.

Reflections on the Words of Jesus

Did you know that as much as 70 percent of a woman's body weight is made up of water? If that amount falls by only 5 percent, she might find it difficult to move and think clearly. If it decreases by more than 10 percent, she could die.

Water sustains life. This is true for your physical body and also for your spirit. Jesus' gift of "living water" represents the cleansing of your heart from sin and the gift of eternal life. Without it, you would literally die of spiritual thirst.

God has placed the well of living water within your reach. All you have to do is drink—by surrendering your heart to him—and eternal life will be yours. And you can also choose to enjoy refreshing sips of living water throughout the day. Talk to God. Read his word. Worship him. Drink in great draughts of his life-giving presence.

One Final Thought

One drink from the living water God offers will quench your spiritual thirst and sustain you in this life as well as in the life to come.

A Drink of Living Water

God's gift has restored our relationship with him and given us back our lives. And there's more life to come—an eternity of life!   Titus 3:7 THE MESSAGE

Jesus said to her, "I am the resurrection and the life. Those who believe in me, even though they die, will live, and everyone who lives and believes in me will never die.

John 11:25–26 NRSV

Whoever believes in the Son has eternal life.

John 3:36 NRSV

The wages of sin is death, but the gift of God is eternal life in Christ Jesus our Lord.

Romans 6:23 NIV

It is necessary for the Son of Man to be lifted up—and everyone who looks up to him, trusting and expectant, will gain a real life, eternal life.

John 3:14–15 THE MESSAGE

God has given us eternal life, and this life is in His Son.   1 John 5:11 NKJV

Eternity is not something that begins after you are dead. It is going on all the time. We are in it now.

Charlotte Gilman

"Eternal life" is the sole sanction for the values of this life.

Dorothy L. Sayers

The real meaning of eternal life is a life that can face anything it has to face without wavering.

Oswald Chambers

We see in the Risen Christ the end for which man was made and the assurance that the end is within reach.

Author Unknown

The life of faith does not earn eternal life; it is eternal life. And Christ is its vehicle. William Temple

Seems it strange that thou shouldst live forever? Is it any less strange that thou shouldst live at all? This is a miracle; and that no more.

Edward Young

When ten thousand times ten thousand times ten thousand years have passed, eternity will have just begun.

Billy Sunday

Full and Overflowing

When Jesus had finished
speaking, he said to Simon,
"Put out into the deep
water and let down your
nets for a catch."
Luke 5:4 NRSV

The Story Behind What Jesus Said

Discouragement filled Simon Peter's heart. He'd fished all night, yet had returned to shore without a single catch. As soon as he scrubbed his nets, Peter was headed for home. But Jesus stopped him, asking to use Peter's boat as a floating pulpit to speak to the growing crowds. Peter agreed immediately and put out a little way from the shore.

After Jesus finished teaching, he instructed Peter to go fishing—again. Peter protested, yet Jesus persisted. Grudgingly, Peter gave in to Jesus' seemingly useless request. Soon Peter's net overflowed with so many fish that his boat almost sank beneath the weight of the catch. Peter fell to his knees, awestruck by his own weakness in light of Jesus' perfect power.

Reflections on the Words of Jesus

You may remember many occasions when a young friend or sibling asked to borrow your favorite toy when you were a little girl. You may or may not have agreed. However, if your mother or father asked for that toy—even without explaining the reasons behind their request—you probably handed it over to your parent without hesitation.

Obedience to God works much the same way. Just as you respect and obey your mother and father, you respect and obey God. You obey because of who is asking, not because you always fully understand the whys behind his request. You obey out of deference to his power and authority.

The more you trust and respect God, the easier it is to obey him. The more you obey him, the more frequently you'll find yourself face-to-face with the magnificent reality of how amazing God—and his goodness toward you—really is.

One Final Thought

Obeying God is more about relationship than "rule following." The deeper your relationship with him, the easier it will be to obey him and reap the benefits of that obedience.

Full and Overflowing

This is the love of God, that we keep His commandments. And His commandments are not burdensome. For whatever is born of God overcomes the world. 1 John 5:3–4 NKJV

LORD, during the night I remember who you are. That's why I keep your law.

Psalm 119:55 NIrV

Those who obey God's word really do love him. That is the way to know whether or not we live in him. Those who say they live in God should live their lives as Christ did.

1 John 2:5–6 NLT

[Jesus said:] "As the Father has loved me, so I have loved you; abide in my love. If you keep my commandments, you will abide in my love, just as I have kept my Father's commandments and abide in his love.

John 15:9–10 NRSV

Once made perfect, [Jesus] became the source of eternal salvation for all who obey him.

Hebrews 5:9 NIV

God is working in you, giving you the desire to obey him and the power to do what pleases him.

Philippians 2:13 NLT

The surest evidence of our love to Christ is obedience to the laws of Christ. Love is the root, obedience is the fruit.

Matthew Henry

The evidence of knowing God is obeying God.

Eric Alexander

The best measure of a spiritual life is not its ecstasies but its obedience.

Oswald Chambers

Obedience to God is the most infallible evidence of sincere and supreme love to him.

Nathanael Emmons

To know God is to experience His love in Christ, and to return that love in obedience. C. H. Dodd

The Christian must aim at that complete obedience to God in which life finds its highest happiness, its greatest good, its perfect consummation, its peace.

William Barclay

To believe in God is to know that all the rules will be fair and that there will be wonderful surprises.

Newbetti

A Better Way

Jesus said, "I say to you, Love your enemies and pray for those who perse- cute you, so that you may be children of your Father in heaven."

Matthew 5:44–45 NRSV

The Story Behind What Jesus Said

As crowds were gathering to hear the words of the wise teacher from Nazareth, Jesus guided his disciples up a hillside for a private lesson. They were most likely expecting words of power and authority, justice and retribution—something about how Jesus would take his rightful place as the Messiah. Surprise must have registered on their faces when Jesus applauded the meek and urged them to turn the other cheek when wronged.

Then Jesus spoke about "love" and "enemies"—a concept that seemed quite impossible. Jesus explained that by choosing to show love to their enemies, the disciples would be true sons and daughters of their heavenly Father—who had chosen to love them long before they'd ever loved him.

Reflections on the Words of Jesus

Do you have any enemies? At first thought, this may sound ridiculous. After all, you're just a normal, kind-hearted, God-fearing woman. Crime bosses have enemies. Dictators have enemies. But you? You probably just have a handful of people you don't get along with or who rub you the wrong way. Whatever your story happens to be, when you run into any of these people on the street, *love* probably isn't the first word that pops into your mind.

It should be. Let the faces of those who make you feel uncomfortable be your catalyst to prayer. Pray for them personally, for your relationship, and for ideas on how to reach out to them in love.

This probably strikes you as unnatural. That's just the point. Choosing to love someone you don't *feel* love for takes something supernatural. It takes the power of God. God's love working through you has the power to transform an enemy into a friend.

One Final Thought

Love is a choice, not simply a feeling. Praying for those who may seem unlovable is the first step toward turning dislike or hatred into love.

A Better Way

If your enemies are hungry, give them bread to eat; and if they are thirsty, give them water to drink.   Proverbs 25:21 NRSV

Put away from you all bitterness and wrath and anger and wrangling and slander, together with all malice, and be kind to one another, tenderhearted, forgiving one another, as God in Christ has forgiven you.

Ephesians 4:31–32 NRSV

When we please the LORD, even our enemies make friends with us.

Proverbs 16:7 CEV

Walk in love, as Christ also has loved us and given Himself for us.

Ephesians 5:2 NKJV

Don't copy the behavior and customs of this world, but let God transform you into a new person by changing the way you think. Then you will know what God wants you to do.

Romans 12:2 NLT

Bless those who curse you, pray for those who mistreat you.   Luke 6:28 NIV

Christian love is an attitude, not a feeling.
Joseph Fletcher

You never so touch the ocean of God's love as when you forgive and love your enemies.
Corrie ten Boom

Pour into me such love for you and for all that any hatred and bitterness may be blotted out.
Dietrich Bonhoeffer

I have decided to stick with love. Hate is too great a burden to bear.
Martin Luther King Jr.

Do good to your friend to keep him, to your enemy to gain him. Benjamin Franklin

There is only one true way of conquering enemies in this warring world, and that is to make your enemy your friend.
Father Andrew

We should conduct ourselves toward our enemy as if he were one day to be our friend.
John Henry Newman

United in Purpose

> Looking at those who sat around him, Jesus said, "Here are my mother and my brothers! Whoever does the will of God is my brother and sister and mother."
>
> Mark 3:34–35 NRSV

The Story Behind What Jesus Said

Healing the hurting, teaching the spiritually hungry, facing persecution from Jewish religious leaders . . . the demands on Jesus grew right along with his popularity. Constantly surrounded by needy, inquisitive, often angry crowds, Jesus and his disciples were so busy they sometimes couldn't find time to eat. Jesus' family, perhaps fearing for his safety, came to the place where he was speaking and called to him.

Yet Jesus knew what his Father wanted him to do—and he was determined to do it. When his mother and brothers asked to speak to him privately, Jesus redefined who his family really was. Deeper than biological ties were the spiritual ties that bound Jesus to those who also chose to follow his true Father's will.

Jesus loved and respected his mother and siblings. He didn't overlook them, but he saw beyond them to a higher purpose— the one for which God, his heavenly Father, had sent him.

God has a plan and purpose for your life just as he did for Jesus' life—a plan that transcends even the most ambitious and well-intentioned hopes and concerns your mother, father, sisters, and brothers might have had for you. That plan defines what you were created to do and to be.

It's particularly easy for a woman to become sidetracked because she often serves as a caregiver to her family. Your family is important to God, and he is honored when you care for them. Be sure, however, that you listen for God's voice in the midst of it all. When your life honors God's will, it will honor your earthly family as well.

One Final Thought

When you seek God's will as the primary focus of your life, you become a cherished part of God's eternal family.

Timeless Wisdom for Everyday Living

United in Purpose

My Father's will is that everyone who looks to the Son and believes in him shall have eternal life, and I will raise him up at the last day.

John 6:40 NIV

The world and its desire are passing away, but those who do the will of God live forever.

1 John 2:17 NRSV

You do not know what will happen tomorrow. For what is your life? It is even a vapor that appears for a little time and then vanishes away. Instead you ought to say, "If the Lord wills, we shall live and do this or that."

James 4:14–15 NKJV

Always pursue what is good both for yourselves and for all. Rejoice always, pray without ceasing, in everything give thanks; for this is the will of God in Christ Jesus for you.

1 Thessalonians 5:15–18 NKJV

I delight to do your will, O my God; your law is within my heart.

Psalm 40:8 NRSV

"I want your will, not mine."   Luke 22:42 NLT

All moral obligation resolves itself into the obligation of conformity to the will of God.

Charles Hodge

There is no peace but in the will of God. God's will is our peace and there is no other peace.

Saint Augustine of Hippo

There are no disappointments to those whose wills are buried in the will of God.

Frederick William Faber

No one may prefer his own will to the will of God, but in everything we must seek and do the will of God.

Saint Basil

The center of God's will is our only safety. Betsie ten Boom

All heaven is waiting to help those who will discover the will of God and do it.

J. Robert Ashcroft

The end of life is not to deny self, nor to be true, nor to keep the Ten Commandments—it is simply to do God's will.

Henry Drummond

A Good Measure

Jesus said, "Forgive, and you will be forgiven. Give, and it will be given to you. A good measure, pressed down, shaken together and running over, will be poured into your lap."
Luke 6:37–38 NIV

The Story Behind What Jesus Said

The disciples had been criticized, ridiculed, and persecuted right along with Jesus. Yet Jesus encouraged them to respond with mercy, forgiveness, and generosity. This wasn't the old law of "an eye for an eye." This was a new way of showering others with blessing beyond what their actions seemed to deserve.

Jesus promised that the disciples' generosity would not go unrewarded, even if those the disciples poured out their love on did not respond in kind. When Jesus said these blessings would be "poured into your lap," he referred to the fold in the disciples' robes that they held up to use as a pocket when they needed to carry things. Their blessings would be more than they could hold.

Jesus presented his disciples with a radical concept—throw judgment and condemnation out the window and replace them with forgiveness and generosity.

The reason Jesus discouraged his disciples from judging others wasn't because their malicious deeds were undeserving of being judged. People will be judged—only not by his disciples or by you. God is the only one wise enough to give people what they truly deserve. Through Jesus' sacrifice, God offered everyone what no one deserves—an unconditional pardon.

As a woman, you will have many opportunities to extend mercy, rather than judgment—when your neighbor asks you to baby-sit again, when your child puts a dent in the fender of your car, or when your husband fails to keep a promise. And when you do extend mercy, you are treating others as God treats you.

One Final Thought

Choosing to respond to others with a generous measure of love and forgiveness rather than judgment pleases God and allows him to pour out his blessings on you.

Timeless Wisdom for Everyday Living

A Good Measure

Let us not judge one another anymore, but rather resolve this, not to put a stumbling block or a cause to fall in our brother's way.   Romans 14:13 NKJV

Most important of all, continue to show deep love for each other, for love covers a multitude of sins.

1 Peter 4:8 NLT

Add to your faith virtue; and to virtue knowledge; and to knowledge temperance; and to temperance patience, and to patience godliness, and to godliness brotherly kindness; and to brotherly kindness charity.

2 Peter 1:7 KJV

You are the people of God; he loved you and chose you for his own. So then, you must clothe yourselves with compassion, kindness, humility, gentleness, and patience. Be tolerant with one another and forgive one another whenever any of you has a complaint against someone else. You must forgive one another just as the Lord has forgiven you.

Colossians 3:12–13 GNT

When you judge others and then do the same things which they do, you condemn yourself.

Romans 2:1 GNT

He has the right to criticize who has the heart to help.
Abraham Lincoln

God himself, sir, does not propose to judge a man until his life is over. Why should you and I?
Samuel Johnson

Do not think of the faults of others but of what is good in them and faulty in yourself.
Saint Teresa of Avila

How rarely we weigh our neighbor in the same balance in which we weigh ourselves.
Thomas à Kempis

The business of finding fault is very easy, and that of doing better very difficult. Saint Francis of Sales

No man can justly censure or condemn another because no man truly knows another.
Sir Thomas Browne

When it seems that God shows us the faults of others, keep on the safer side. It may be that thy judgment is false.
Saint Catherine of Siena

From the Heart

Jesus said, "It is out of the
abundance of the heart that
the mouth speaks."

Luke 6:45 NRSV

The Story Behind What Jesus Said

People from Judea mingled with those from Jerusalem. Travelers
from the distant seacoasts of Tyre and Sidon sat alongside
people whose only experience with the sea was fishing on a lake
near Galilee. To teach such a diverse crowd, Jesus may have been
looking for common ground. So he chose an analogy that everyone could understand.

Jesus' listeners knew apple trees consistently bore apples.
Grapevines bore grapes. An unhealthy tree would bear unhealthy
fruit. So Jesus likened the human heart to a fruit tree and words
to the fruit it produced. He explained that what grew in people's
hearts was evident by what came out of their mouths. Smooth
words couldn't disguise an evil heart. The fruit's true nature
would always be revealed.

Reflections on the Words of Jesus

Your physical heart may be hidden from view, but its nature is revealed by how well your body is working. A healthy heart keeps your blood pumping regularly. An unhealthy heart will reveal itself through a variety of symptoms, some of them fatal.

Your metaphorical heart, the core of who you really are, works much the same way. If your heart is pure, continually cleansed by God's grace and forgiveness, your words will reveal what's going on inside. Your speech will be pure and clean. What you say won't carry any contagion that could potentially harm others. Instead it will be filled with wholesome encouragement, praise, gentleness, and truth.

Talking is one of the things women love to do most when they get together. Pay attention to what you say. Your words will reveal the condition of your heart. Then you and God can work together to keep it healthy.

One Final Thought

What comes out of your mouth begins in your heart. Inviting God to purge the deepest corners of your heart will purify your speech and transform your life.

Timeless Wisdom for Everyday Living

From the Heart

Wash me thoroughly from my guilt, and cleanse me from my sin. . . . Create a clean heart in me, O God, and renew a faithful spirit within me.

Psalm 51:2, 10 GOD'S WORD

How can young people keep their way pure? By guarding it according to your word.

Psalm 119:9 NRSV

Who may climb the LORD's hill or stand in his holy temple? Only those who do right for the right reasons, and don't worship idols or tell lies under oath.

Psalm 24:3–4 CEV

Blessed are the pure in heart, for they shall see God.

Matthew 5:8 NASB

The blood of Christ will purify our hearts from deeds that lead to death so that we can worship the living God. For by the power of the eternal Spirit, Christ offered himself to God as a perfect sacrifice for our sins.

Hebrews 9:14 NLT

Wash me, and I shall be whiter than snow.

Psalm 51:7 NASB

No man or woman can really be strong, gentle, pure, and good without the world being better for it.

Phillips Brooks

The pure soul is a beautiful rose, and the Three Divine persons descend from Heaven to inhale its fragrance.

Saint John Vianney

Spiritual truth is discernible only to a pure heart, not to a keen intellect. It is not a question of profundity of intellect, but of purity of heart.

Oswald Chambers

If there is joy in the world, surely the man of pure heart possesses it.

Thomas à Kempis

How to be pure? By longing for the one good, that is, God. Meister Eckhart

Let us always remember that holiness does not consist in doing uncommon things, but in doing everything with purity of heart.

Henry Edward Manning

Holiness is not the laborious acquisition of virtue from without, but the expression of the Christ-life from within.

John William Wand

Giving in Secret

Jesus said, "When you give to someone, don't tell your left hand what your right hand is doing. Give your gifts in secret, and your Father, who knows all secrets, will reward you."

Matthew 6:3–4 NLT

The Story Behind What Jesus Said

The disciples watched the crowds flocking to the Galilean hillside. Although Jesus' teaching and miracles were what drew people from miles around, the disciples probably enjoyed being so close to the center of attention. After all, they were the chosen twelve. People were watching them, as well as their Master.

Knowing the appeal of public recognition, Jesus spoke to those closest to him about the danger of doing good deeds just to build themselves up in the eyes of others. He challenged his disciples to give humbly and secretly so that their acts of charity would glorify God, not themselves. God would see what they did, even if others did not. God's pleasure was worth much more than human admiration.

Reflections on the Words of Jesus

When Jesus spoke to his disciples, he didn't challenge them on their generosity. He said *"when* you give," not *"if* you give." Benevolence was an accepted part of the Jewish religion. Alms were given to benefit the temple. Money and aid were given to help widows and the poor.

The need is just as great today as it was when Jesus walked the earth. So is the importance of being motivated by compassion rather than by a desire to appear godly in front of others.

God designed a woman's heart with an affinity to nurture and take care of others. Follow that innate desire. Give generously of your time, your resources, and your abilities—but be stingy with your words when it comes to mentioning what you've done. Give when others aren't looking. Help out in situations where no one knows your name. Praise God each time he provides an opportunity where you can provide for someone else.

One Final Thought

God knows every good gift you give in secret. Let God's delight in what you've done be all the thanks you need.

Timeless Wisdom for Everyday Living

Giving in Secret

Don't forget to do good and to share what you have with those in need, for such sacrifices are very pleasing to God.   Hebrews 13:16 NLT

Whoever gives to the poor will lack nothing.

Proverbs 28:27 NRSV

I tell you, love your enemies. Help and give without expecting a return. You'll never—I promise—regret it. Live out this God-created identity the way our Father lives toward us, generously and graciously, even when we're at our worst.

Luke 6:35 THE MESSAGE

I want each of you to take plenty of time to think it over, and make up your own mind what you will give. That will protect you against sob stories and arm-twisting. God loves it when the giver delights in the giving.

2 Corinthians 9:7 THE MESSAGE

Your father sees what you do in private. He will reward you.

Matthew 6:18 GOD'S WORD

Those who are generous are blessed, for they share their bread with the poor.

Proverbs 22:9 NRSV

There is no happiness in having and getting, but only in giving. Half the world is on the wrong scent in the pursuit of happiness.

F. W. Gunsaulus

Bread for myself is a material question; bread for my neighbor is a spiritual question.

Jacques Maritain

Blessed are those who can give without remembering and take without forgetting.

Elizabeth Bibesco

The world says, "The more you take, the more you have." Christ says, "The more you give, the more you are."

Frederick Buechner

The Bible idea of sacrifice is that I give as a love-gift the very best thing I have. Oswald Chambers

Who gives to the poor, lends to God.

Spanish Proverb

A cheerful giver does not count the cost of what he gives. His heart is set on pleasing and cheering him to whom the gift is given.

Julian of Norwich

51

A Solitary Place

Jesus said, "Let us go off by ourselves to some place where we will be alone and you can rest a while."

Mark 6:31 GNT

The Story Behind What Jesus Said

With God's help, the disciples healed the sick and cast out demons, just as Jesus said they would. Their success, along with Jesus' increasing celebrity, drew larger crowds than ever before. Jesus and the disciples hardly had a minute to themselves. There was always someone in need.

Yet they, too, were in need. Physically, they were pushed to the limit—they were so busy they often missed meals and got little sleep. Emotionally, they were grieving the execution of John the Baptist. Spiritually, they needed to constantly refocus on God, instead of the miracles happening around them. Jesus knew the disciples' needs, just as he did those of the crowd. It wouldn't take a miracle to heal them. All they needed was time away to rest.

When children go beyond their limits, they need a time-out. Something in their life is out of control—their words, their actions, or their emotions. A time-out helps them calm down, refocus, and start over.

Even adults need a time-out now and then. Jesus saw that need in his disciples. They were overworked, stressed, not taking care of themselves physically. That may sound familiar to you. It's easy to let the busyness of life, even the desire to do good, push you beyond your physical and emotional limits.

When that happens, put yourself in time-out. Take a mini-trip to the wilderness by taking a walk, singing worship songs in the tub, or sitting still and enjoying God's presence. Whatever you choose to do, realign yourself with God and reestablish healthy limits in your daily habits. Every woman needs balance to maintain the multiple roles she pursues. So follow Jesus' example.

One Final Thought

The busier your schedule, the more important it becomes to take some time to rest and recuperate in God's arms.

Timeless Wisdom for Everyday Living

I fall asleep in peace the moment I lie down because you alone, O LORD, enable me to live securely.   Psalm 4:8 GOD'S WORD

I lay down and slept. I woke up in safety, for the LORD was watching over me.
Psalm 3:5 NLT

Come to Me, all who are weary and heavy-laden, and I will give you rest. Take My yoke upon you and learn from Me, for I am gentle and humble in heart; and you will find rest for your souls.
Matthew 11:28–29 NASB

Yet, the strength of those who wait with hope in the LORD will be renewed. They will soar on wings like eagles. They will run and won't become weary. They will walk and won't grow tired.
Isaiah 40:31 GOD'S WORD

Be at rest once more, O my soul, for the LORD has been good to you.
Psalm 116:7 NIV

All who enter into God's rest will find rest from their labors, just as God rested after creating the world.   Hebrews 4:10 NLT

Only in a quiet mind is adequate perception of the world.

Hans Margolius

Let us not go faster than God. It is our emptiness and our thirst that he needs, not our plenitude.

Jacques Maritain

All the troubles of life come upon us because we refuse to sit quietly for a while each day in our room.

Blaise Pascal

True silence is the rest of the mind and is to the spirit what sleep is to the body, nourishment and refreshment.

William Penn

You have made us for yourself, and our hearts are restless till they find their rest in you. Saint Augustine of Hippo

Jesus knows we must come apart and rest awhile, or else we may just plain come apart.

Vance Havner

If we possess inward solitude, we will not fear being alone, for we know that we are not alone.

Richard J. Foster

Say the Word

Jesus turned around and said
to the crowd following him,
"I tell you, I have never
found faith like this, not even
in Israel!"

Luke 7:9 GNT

The Story Behind What Jesus Said

A Jewish slave lay ill and close to death. Jesus being asked to heal
him wasn't out of the ordinary. However, the fact that the request
came from a Roman officer was. The officer hadn't come in person. A powerful man of great authority, he sent someone else to
do his bidding, a Jew who might relate more easily to Jesus
than he.

The officer didn't request that Jesus come quickly. He acknowl-
edged that as a man of authority like him, Jesus surely could have
his bidding accomplished with just a word—if he spoke, the
slave would be healed. Jesus was amazed at the man's depth of
faith and understanding of his power. He praised the officer's
faith and healed his slave.

Reflections on the Words of Jesus

Faith alone can't move mountains. It's only when you act on what you believe that God's power is unleashed in your life. That action may be as simple as asking God for help, as the Roman officer did on behalf of his slave. Or it may be as difficult as forgiving someone who has hurt you despite that person's unrepentant spirit.

Believing that God loves you, that he created you for a unique purpose, that he is actively involved in what goes on in this world, and that he can bring good out of every circumstance is important. Unless you let what you believe change your life, however, your faith is nothing more than mental gymnastics.

Put your faith into action today. Ask God to help you apply what he reveals to you through his word, prayer, and the godly advice of those around you. Let him lead you to the mountains and show you how to tackle them.

One Final Thought

A true woman of faith acts on what she believes, letting God's power transform her life, her mind, and her heart.

Timeless Wisdom for Everyday Living

Say the Word

Remember your leaders who have spoken God's word to you. Think about how their lives turned out, and imitate their faith. Hebrews 13:7 GOD'S WORD

The act of faith is what distinguished our ancestors, set them above the crowd.

Hebrews 11:2 THE MESSAGE

As you share the faith you have in common with others, I pray that you may come to have a complete knowledge of every blessing we have in Christ.

Philemon 1:6 GOD'S WORD

If you have faith as small as a mustard seed, you can say to this mountain, "Move from here to there" and it will move. Nothing will be impossible for you.

Matthew 17:20 NIV

Just as the body is dead without a spirit, so also faith is dead without good deeds.

James 2:26 NLT

Anyone who has faith in me [Jesus] will do what I have been doing. John 14:12 NIV

Faith is an act of rational choice, which determines us to act as if certain things were true.

William R. Inge

Works without faith are like a fish without water: It wants the element it should live in.

Owen Feltham

Faith is the root of works. A root that produces nothing is dead.

Thomas Wilson

As the flower is before the fruit, so is faith before good works.

Richard Whatley

He that is without faith is without works; and he that is without works is without faith. Charles Spurgeon

The greatest danger for faith continues to be the divorce between faith and life with its commitments.

Juan Luis Segundo

You do right when you offer faith to God; you do right when you offer works. But if you separate the two, then you do wrong.

Saint Bernard of Clairvaux

59

Spirit and Truth

Jesus said, "A time is coming and has now come when the true worshipers will worship the Father in spirit and truth, for they are the kind of worshipers the Father seeks."
John 4:23 NIV

The Story Behind What Jesus Said

As the conversation at the well continued, the Samaritan woman became increasingly uncomfortable and curious about the stranger she was speaking to. How had he found out that she had had five husbands and was currently living with a man who wasn't one of them? The woman quickly changed the subject of their conversation from her personal life to a hotly debated religious topic—the proper place to worship God.

Jesus wasn't interested in debating religion or morality. He shifted the conversation back to what really mattered—God himself. He explained that true worship wasn't dependent on where a person was physically, but spiritually. God's Spirit was everywhere, available to everyone who willingly accepted the truth about his son.

JESUS SPEAKS TO WOMEN

Reflections on the Words of Jesus

Worship is a loving response to an encounter with a holy God. In the Bible, people fell on their faces, burst into song, built temples, danced with abandon, gave their last coin, and moved forward in obedience when they came face-to-face with the God of the universe. These people honored God with their actions and attitudes.

The how of worship is always secondary to the who. Throughout the day God's fundamental question—"Who do you say I am?"—echoes through your life. When your answer is in line with God's own, worship happens.

Intentionally refocusing on God more often will increase your daily worship time. Whether you're blow-drying your hair, paying bills, or contemplating getting on that exercise bike, recognize that every moment offers an opportunity to look at God more closely. Then respond with awe and obedience to what you see.

One Final Thought

No building can contain God. He is everywhere you are, waiting to respond to your true worship as you honor him with your actions and attitudes.

Spirit and Truth

Since we are receiving a kingdom that cannot be shaken, let us give thanks, by which we offer to God an acceptable worship with reverence and awe. Hebrews 12:28 NRSV

Shout with joy to the LORD, O earth! Worship the LORD with gladness. Come before him, singing with joy. Acknowledge that the LORD is God! He made us, and we are his. We are his people, the sheep of his pasture.

Psalm 100:1–3 NLT

Great is the LORD and most worthy of praise; he is to be feared above all gods.

1 Chronicles 16:25 NIV

Ascribe to the LORD the glory due his name; worship the LORD in the splendor of his holiness.

Psalm 29:2 NIV

I appeal to you therefore, brothers and sisters, by the mercies of God, to present your bodies as a living sacrifice, holy and acceptable to God, which is your spiritual worship.

Romans 12:1 NRSV

O come, let us worship and bow down, let us kneel before the Lord, our Maker! Psalm 95:6 NRSV

If worship does not change us, it has not been worship.
Richard Foster

The worship of God is not a rule of safety—it is an adventure of the spirit.
Alfred North Whitehead

Worship then is not a part of the Christian life; it is the Christian life.
Gerald Vann

Worship is the celebration of life in its totality. Worship is the festival of creation.
William Stringfellow

One act of inward worship are prayers which, however short, are nevertheless acceptable to God. Brother Lawrence

Worship can only truly express joy, sorrow, hope, faith, and love if it is firmly rooted in the actual lives and experience of the people who are worshiping.
Ianthe Pratt

There is only one perfect act of worship ever offered and that was the life of Jesus Christ himself.
Herbert M. Carson

Treasure in Heaven

Jesus said, "Take care! Be on your guard against all kinds of greed; for one's life does not consist in the abundance of possessions."

Luke 12:15 NRSV

The Story Behind What Jesus Said

The man forced his way through the crowd toward Jesus. Surely this great religious Teacher would understand how greedy his brother was and make him share their father's estate. Jesus recognized that the man's own greed was as great as his brother's. Instead of settling a financial dispute, Jesus told him a story.

Once upon a time, there was a man rich in land and crops. But he still wasn't satisfied. He built bigger barns, hoping to stockpile even more of his wealth. He promised himself that he'd rest once he acquired enough. That day never came. The man died that very night and was chastised by God for being a fool who valued earthly riches over a rich relationship with God.

Reflections on the Words of Jesus

Materialism is like a top-ten country tune. More often than not, it starts off with the promise of happiness but winds up in dashed dreams, broken hearts, loneliness, and tragedy. It may sound melodramatic, but falling in love with what money can buy will lead you down that very same path.

That's because the things that have price tags are temporal—a sumptuous dinner, that new pair of shoes, a custom-built home, the sleekest sports car, even the diamond in your wedding ring. Contrary to marketing pitches, diamonds aren't really forever, you know. Things simply aren't designed to last. Only God and people are.

The abundant wealth found in relationship with God and others—the joy of experiencing God's love, the hope of eternal life, supernatural peace in turbulent times, and much more—cannot be taken from you. These treasures are the eternal riches of God.

One Final Thought

Choose to invest your life, your time, and your love in what lasts, instead of what wears out, breaks down, or loses value.

Treasure in Heaven

Command those who are rich in this present age not to be haughty, nor to trust in uncertain riches but in the living God.   1 Timothy 6:17 NKJV

Some pretend to be rich, yet have nothing; others pretend to be poor, yet have great wealth.

Proverbs 13:7 NRSV

Better one handful with tranquillity than two handfuls with toil and chasing after the wind.

Ecclesiastes 4:6 NIV

There is nothing on earth that I desire other than you. My flesh and my heart may fail, but God is the strength of my heart and my portion forever.

Psalm 73:25–26 NRSV

Don't hoard treasure down here where it gets eaten by moths and corroded by rust or—worse!—stolen by burglars. Stockpile treasure in heaven, where it's safe from moth and rust and burglars.

Matthew 6:19–20 THE MESSAGE

We brought nothing into the world, and we can take nothing out of it.   1 Timothy 6:7 NIV

Happiness doesn't depend on the actual number of blessings we manage to scratch from life, but on our attitude toward them.

Alexander Solzhenitsyn

Treasures in heaven are accumulated by our attitude to our treasures (or lack of them) on earth.

Erwin W. Lutzer

If any person, because of his state of life, cannot do without wealth and position, let him at least keep his heart empty of love of them.

Saint Angela Merici

The real measure of our wealth is how much we'd be worth if we lost all our money.

John Henry Jowell

To dispense wealth is the best way to preserve it. Isaac Barrow

As riches grow, care follows, and a thirst for more and more.

Horace

In this world it is not what we take up, but what we give up that makes us rich.

Henry Ward Beecher

Nothing to Eat

Jesus called his disciples to him and said, "I have compassion for these people; they have already been with me three days and have nothing to eat."

Mark 8:1–2 NIV

The Story Behind What Jesus Said

They came out of curiosity, Jews and Gentiles alike. Some had traveled long distances, while others lived right there on the Sea of Galilee. Yet none of them had expected to spend three whole days just listening to Jesus. When Jesus looked at the crowd, he saw people who were not only hungry for God but also for food.

Jesus' compassion led him to action. All that remained of the disciples' provisions were seven loaves of bread. Jesus took the bread, along with a few fish gathered from the crowd. After blessing the food, Jesus passed the meager meal out to the more than four thousand people. Not only did everyone eat his fill, the disciples collected seven baskets of leftovers. Another miracle had occurred.

Reflections on the Words of Jesus

The world is filled with needs even more overwhelming than providing food for thousands—the AIDS epidemic in Africa, child prostitution in Thailand, starvation that reaches around the globe, the homeless in your own hometown. You don't have the power to solve all the world's problems.

But that is the lesson Jesus taught on the day he fed so many. Rather than deny the compassion he was feeling, Jesus took what was available (bread and a few fish) and passed it out to the people. Provisions would be multiplied to meet the need.

As you feel your heart filling with compassion for the great needs around you, ask God to show you what you can do to meet the need. That may mean reaching out to someone who needs a helping hand. Then pray that God will bless and multiply your efforts on behalf of a needy world.

One Final Thought

When you look with compassion on the needs around you, ask God to bless and multiply what you can do to meet those needs.

Timeless Wisdom for Everyday Living

Nothing to Eat

The LORD longs to be gracious to you; he rises to show you compassion. For the LORD is a God of justice. Blessed are all who wait for him!

Isaiah 30:18 NIV

Be kind and compassionate to one another, forgiving each other, just as in Christ God forgave you.

Ephesians 4:32 NIV

Through the LORD's mercies we are not consumed, because His compassions fail not. They are new every morning; Great is Your faithfulness. "The LORD is my portion," says my soul, "Therefore I hope in Him!"

Lamentations 3:22–24 NKJV

Chosen by God for this new life of love, dress in the wardrobe God picked out for you: compassion, kindness, humility, quiet strength, discipline. Be even-tempered, content with second place, quick to forgive an offense.

Colossians 3:12 THE MESSAGE

All of you, have unity of spirit, sympathy, love for one another, a tender heart, and a humble mind.

1 Peter 3:8 NRSV

The Lord is good to everyone. He showers compassion on all his creation. Psalm 145:9 NLT

There is no wilderness so terrible, so beautiful, so arid, so fruitful, as the wilderness of compassion. It is the only desert that shall truly flourish like a lily.

Thomas Merton

I would rather make mistakes in kindness and compassion than work miracles in unkindness and hardness.

Mother Teresa

God does not comfort us to make us comfortable, but to make us comforters.

John Henry Jowett

Compassion is hard because it requires the inner disposition to go with others to the place where they are weak, vulnerable, lonely, and broken.

Henry Nouwen

The dew of compassion is a tear.

Lord Byron

Christ did not separate himself from human beings and their needs. Nor did he limit his concern to the spiritual part of man's personality.

Erwin W. Lutzer

Every act of kindness and compassion done by any man for his fellow Christian is done by Christ working within him.

Julian of Norwich

Well Done

Jesus said, "Well done, good and faithful servant! You have been faithful with a few things; I will put you in charge of many things. Come and share your master's happiness!"
Matthew 25:21 NIV

The Story Behind What Jesus Said

Jesus had a lot to say to his disciples and not a lot of time left to say it. Things were heating up, and plots were being contrived. It would be no more than a few days before the final events of his life would play themselves out.

Leaving the temple for what he knew would be the last time, Jesus took his disciples to a quiet hillside near the Mount of Olives. There, speaking in parables, he told them what he could about what was to come. And he urged them to remain watchful and focused, continuing to do what they had seen him do until the day when he would return and reward them personally for their faithfulness.

Reflections on the Words of Jesus

"Well done, good and faithful servant!" is a phrase that many people toss around. Perhaps they assume that Jesus was referring to the person who lived a successful and productive life, someone who made a difference in this world or had laudable achievements. "Well done," God would say. "Good job!"

Jesus wasn't talking about achievement at all. Faithfulness was the focus of his remarks. He wanted his followers to know that one day they would be applauded for remaining true to God and their calling during the difficult times ahead.

Faithfulness is the primary standard God applies to your life as well. What it takes to win his approval, his pat-on-the-back endorsement, is for you to be the kind of woman who keeps moving forward, stays the course, and uses the gifts you've been given to the fullest—until the day he enthusiastically welcomes you home with the words, "Good job, my faithful servant!"

One Final Thought

People celebrate achievement, but the characteristic that merits God's highest approval is keeping the faith and doing what he's called you to do until you meet him face-to-face.

Well Done

Let those who love the LORD hate evil. He guards the lives of those who are faithful to him. He saves them from the power of sinful people.

Psalm 97:10 NIrV

It is required that those who have been given a trust must prove faithful.

1 Corinthians 4:2 NIV

When the Holy Spirit controls our lives, he will produce this kind of fruit in us: love, joy, peace, patience, kindness, goodness, faithfulness, gentleness, and self-control. Here there is no conflict with the law.

Galatians 5:22–23 NLT

Let love and faithfulness never leave you; bind them around your neck, write them on the tablet of your heart. Then you will win favor and a good name in the sight of God and man.

Proverbs 3:3–4 NIV

We want each of you to be faithful to the very end. We want you to be sure of what you hope for.

Hebrews 6:11 NIrV

To the faithful you show yourself faithful, to the blameless you show yourself blameless.

Psalm 18:25 NIV

It does not matter whether you preach in Westminster Abbey, or teach a ragged class, so you be faithful. The faithfulness is all.

George Macdonald

The Lord rewards faithfulness above fruitfulness, which puts us all on the same footing, whether famous for our effectiveness or unknown in our faithfulness.

John Piper

It is only by fidelity in little things that a true and constant love of God can be distinguished from a passing fervor of spirit.

François Fénelon

Nothing is more noble, nothing more venerable than fidelity. Faithfulness and truth are the most sacred excellencies and endowments of the human mind.

Cicero

Nobody else can do the work that God marked out for you. Paul Laurence Dunbar

The one dominant note in Jesus' life was to do his Father's will. His is not the way of wisdom or of success, but the way of faithfulness.

Oswald Chambers

God requires a faithful fulfill-ment of the merest trifle given us to do, rather than the most ardent aspiration to things to which we are not called.

Saint Francis of Sales

Set Free

Jesus said to those who believed in him, "If you obey my teaching, you are really my disciples: you will know the truth, and the truth will set you free."

John 8:31–32 GNT

The Story Behind What Jesus Said

Jesus, surrounded by a crowd of eager listeners, had been sitting on the steps of the temple since earliest light. The Pharisees and teachers of the law lurked nearby, looking for an opportunity to challenge him. When Jesus refused to condone the stoning of an adulterous woman they had thrown at his feet, the religious leaders verbally attacked him in earnest.

Their message was clear. They wanted to know just who Jesus thought he was. That was the opening Jesus had been waiting for. Not only did he tell them who he was—the Light of the world, the Son of God—but he also told them who they were—pretenders, slaves to sin, and blind men unable to face the truth.

Reflections on the Words of Jesus

The Pharisees and teachers of the law were so committed to their religious notions that they were blinded to the simple truth. The Son of God, the long-awaited Messiah, was sitting right there on the steps of the temple, and yet they did not recognize him.

A great many people, even in these enlightened times, fail to recognize who Jesus is. They might think of him as a charismatic carpenter, a great teacher, a miracle-worker. If only they could see the truth about him. Jesus is the instrument of salvation to all who are lost. He is the giver of living water; he is the only sacrifice for sin acceptable to God.

When you know the truth about Jesus, you will be free to pursue a life with meaning and eternal purpose. You will be free to love, to hope, and to live in peace. You will be free to become the woman God has created you to be.

One Final Thought

The truth about who Jesus is—God's Son, the Light of the World, the Living Water, the only Sacrifice for Sin—is the truth that frees the human soul.

Timeless Wisdom for Everyday Living

Set Free

It's in Christ that you, once you heard the truth and believed it (this Message of your salvation), found yourselves home free—signed, sealed, and delivered by the Holy Spirit.   Ephesians 1:13 THE MESSAGE

I could have no greater joy than to hear that my children live in the truth.

3 John 1:4 NLT

The Son of God has come and has given us understanding, so that we may know him who is true. And we are in him who is true—even in his Son Jesus Christ.

1 John 5:20 NIV

When the Friend comes, the Spirit of the Truth, he will take you by the hand and guide you into all the truth there is.

John 16:13 THE MESSAGE

Little children, let us not love with word or with tongue, but in deed and truth.

1 John 3:18 NASB

Love does not delight in evil but rejoices with the truth.   1 Corinthians 13:6 NIV

Christianity is not true because it works. It works because it is true.

Os Guinness

Each truth revealed by grace, and received with inward delight and joy, is a secret murmur of God in the ear of a pure soul.

Walter Hilton

It is easier to perceive error than to find truth, for the former lies on the surface . . . while the latter lies in the depth.

Johann Wolfgang von Goethe

It is obvious that to be in earnest in seeking the truth is an indispensable requisite for finding it.

John Henry Newman

Truth is given, not to be contemplated, but to be done. Life is an action, not a thought.

Frederick William Robertson

Any human being can penetrate to the kingdom of truth, if only he longs for truth and perpetually concentrates all his attention upon its attainment.

Simone Weil

Without the Way there is no going; without the Truth there is no knowing; without the Life there is no living.

Thomas à Kempis

Step Out of the Boat

Jesus said, "Take courage!
It is I. Don't be afraid."
Matthew 14:27 NIV

The Story Behind What Jesus Said

John the Baptist was dead—murdered. Jesus and his disciples
hurried to a quiet place where they could rest, pray, and grieve
for their friend. But too quickly the eager crowds found them,
and Jesus couldn't bear to send them away without feeding
them—spiritually and physically. Finally, Jesus could see that his
disciples were exhausted. He urged them to take the boat and
head home while he dismissed the crowd and spent some time
in prayer.

Before dawn, Jesus rejoined his disciples, only to find their boat
floundering in the grip of a dangerous storm. Seeing him walking
toward them on the water, their panic turned to terror. Then
across the waves came their Master's comforting words, "It is I."

Reflections on the Words of Jesus

As a woman, you've probably experienced the sense of exhaustion that comes with the unrelenting demands of family life and the constant knowledge that people are depending on you to be strong and meet their needs. Some days you may feel overwhelmed. Then—just when you think you can't go another step—a bona fide crisis occurs.

Fatigue and discouragement give way to panic, and before you know it you're wondering if Jesus is really the one who can lift you above your circumstances or if he is merely a figment of your imagination. Then through the fear and confusion that surrounds you, you hear those wonderful words, "It is I. Take courage. Don't be afraid."

The power to live your life courageously doesn't come from within. It comes from God. Listen for his voice, and you will be sure to hear it, even over the roar of the storm.

One Final Thought

Life's demands can be overwhelming, but God is always there to give you the courage you need to meet the challenges of each new day.

Timeless Wisdom for Everyday Living

God is our refuge and strength, always ready to help in times of trouble. So we will not fear, even if earthquakes come and the mountains crumble into the sea.   Psalm 46:1–2 NLT

We are not able to claim anything for ourselves. The power to do what we do comes from God.
2 Corinthians 3:5 NIrV

I am confident that I will see the LORD's goodness while I am here in the land of the living. Wait patiently for the LORD. Be brave and courageous. Yes, wait patiently for the LORD.
Psalm 27:13–14 NLT

O love the LORD, all you His godly ones! The LORD preserves the faithful, and fully recompenses the proud doer. Be strong, and let your heart take courage, all you who hope in the LORD.
Psalm 31:23–24 NASB

Do not be so far away, O LORD. Come quickly to help me, O my strength.
Psalm 22:19 GOD'S WORD

Be on your guard. Stand firm in the faith. Be brave. Be strong.   1 Corinthians 16:13 NIrV

Fear can keep a man out of danger, but courage can support him in it.

Thomas Fuller

I shall not fear the battle if thou art by my side, nor wander from the pathway if thou wilt be my guide.

John E. Bode

Give to the winds thy fears; hope and be undismayed: God hears thy sighs and counts thy tears; God shall lift thy head.

Paul Gerhardt

Courage is not simply one of the virtues, but the form of every virtue at the testing point, which means at the point of highest reality.

C. S. Lewis

Courage is fear that has said its prayers. Dorothy Bernard

Fear not, little flock, whatever your lot. He never forsakes; He never is gone, So count on His presence in darkness and dawn.

Paul Rader

Have plenty of courage. God is stronger than the Devil. We are on the winning side.

John Wilbur Chapman

Follow Me

Jesus said, "No one who puts his hand to the plow and looks back is fit for service in the kingdom of God."

Luke 9:62 NIV

The Story Behind What Jesus Said

Jesus' disciples were excited. His ministry was stronger than ever and gaining momentum. They were probably somewhat confused by the urgency in his tone and the power and authority in his words as he announced his decision to return to Jerusalem—a place where he had many dangerous enemies.

The crowds continued to follow Jesus as he walked resolutely toward Jerusalem and the culmination of his earthly mission. "Come be my disciple," he said to individuals in the crowd. But when they said they must go home first to prepare, Jesus warned them that it was too late to look back, too late to tend to business, too late to say goodbye to loved ones. Time was running out. Discipleship had become a now-or-never proposition.

Reflections on the Words of Jesus

Perhaps you've been putting off your commitment to follow Jesus—not because you don't believe he is who he says he is, but because there are things you feel you need to do first—become successful in your career, raise your children, get your personal circumstances under control.

Jesus didn't mean for you to leave your responsibilities behind or neglect your family. The point he was making is that those things should not be used as excuses for failing to commit yourself to a relationship with him.

Preparation in most matters is a good thing, but when it comes to walking with Jesus, no preparation is necessary. All you need do is fall into step behind him. Take too much time to prepare, and you could miss the opportunity entirely. Don't let excuses keep you from a relationship with a God who loves you. Follow Jesus, and do it now.

One Final Thought

Commitment is a "now" proposition. Every day take your stand, follow closely to God, and leave behind any excuses that may slow you down.

Timeless Wisdom for Everyday Living

Follow Me

LORD, teach me how you want me to live. Then I will follow your truth. Give me a heart that doesn't want anything more than to worship you.

Psalm 86:11 NIrV

Commit your way to the LORD.

Psalm 37:5 NASB

[Jesus] called his disciples and the crowds to come over and listen. "If any of you wants to be my follower," he told them, "you must put aside your selfish ambition, shoulder your cross, and follow me."

Mark 8:34 NLT

When you make a vow to God, do not delay fulfilling it; for he has no pleasure in fools. Fulfill what you vow. It is better that you should not vow than that you should vow and not fulfill it.

Ecclesiastes 5:4–5 NRSV

Commit to the LORD whatever you do, and your plans will succeed.

Proverbs 16:3 NIV

My heart is steadfast, O God, my heart is steadfast. Psalm 57:7 NASB

Saviour, 'tis a full surrender,
all I leave to follow Thee;
Thou my Leader and
Defender from this hour shalt
ever be! I surrender all!
Rebecca S. Pollard

Don't touch Christianity
unless you mean business. I
promise you a miserable exis-
tence if you do.
Henry Drummond

Lord, the newness of this day
calls me to an untried way:
Let me gladly take the road.
I will travel through with
Thee.
Henry van Dyke

Lord, take my lips and speak
through them, take my mind
and think through it, take
my heart and set it on fire.
W. H. H. Aitken

He is no fool who gives what he cannot keep to gain what he cannot lose. Jim Elliot

Take my life, and let it be con-
secrated, Lord, to Thee; Take
my moments and my days, let
them flow in ceaseless praise.
Frances Ridley Havergal

To reach the port of heaven we
must sail, sometimes with the
wind and sometimes against
it—but we must sail . . . or lie
at anchor.
Oliver Wendell Holmes

The Good Shepherd

Jesus said, "I am the good shepherd; I know my sheep and my sheep know me—just as the Father knows me and I know the Father—and I lay down my life for the sheep."
John 10:14–15 NIV

The Story Behind What Jesus Said

The Pharisees and teachers of the law followed Jesus everywhere, hoping to catch him breaking the law. But one day, the streets were full of people attending a festival, and Jesus was able to lose himself in the crowd. Away from the Pharisees' prodding eyes, he reached out to a blind man and restored his sight.

When the Pharisees heard the man claiming to have been healed by Jesus, they ridiculed him and threw him out of the temple. Jesus soon arrived at the man's side and a fiery confrontation ensued. Using a parable about sheep, Jesus said that only robbers and thieves destroy the sheep, whereas a true shepherd is willing to lay down his life for them.

The religion that the Pharisees and teachers of the Law were determined to protect consisted of rules and regulations that addressed outward behaviors but could not change hearts. It was a system based on punishing the wrong rather than rewarding the right. It stripped away the life and left only the duty.

The relationship God wants to have with you is not that way at all. Rather, it is built on love and trust and caring. It resembles that of a child with his or her mother or, as Jesus described it, sheep in the tender and constant care of a loving shepherd. He isn't following you around waiting for you to make a mistake. He's busy counting his sheep, comforting them, leading them, protecting them.

Jesus cares for you. He cares so much that he was willing to give his life to pay for all your mistakes and reconnect you with your loving heavenly Father.

One Final Thought

Love fuels your relationship with the Father through his Son Jesus. Under the care of this love, you are liberated and protected.

Timeless Wisdom for Everyday Living

The Good Shepherd

Like a shepherd [the LORD] will tend His flock, in His arm He will gather the lambs and carry them in His bosom; He will gently lead the nursing ewes. Isaiah 40:11 NASB

You were going astray like sheep, but now you have returned to the shepherd and guardian of your souls.

1 Peter 2:25 NRSV

You are my sheep, the sheep of my pasture and I am your God, says the Lord God.

Ezekiel 34:31 NRSV

May [God] produce in you, through the power of Jesus Christ, all that is pleasing to him. Jesus is the great Shepherd of the sheep by an everlasting covenant, signed with his blood. To him be glory forever and ever.

Hebrews 13:21 NLT

The LORD is my Shepherd; I have everything I need. He lets me rest in green meadows; he leads me beside peaceful streams. He renews my strength. He guides me along right paths.

Psalm 23:1–3 NLT

Turn all your worries over to God. He cares about you. 1 Peter 5:7 NIrV

You are our shepherd, and you free us from the snare. You protect us who honour you, O God.

Notker Balbulus

Christ, the Creator of such an enormous universe of overwhelming magnitude, deigns to call Himself my Shepherd and invites me to consider myself His sheep.

Philip Keller

God hears no sweeter music than the cracked chimes of the courageous human spirit ringing in imperfect acknowledgment of his perfect love.

Joshua Loth Liebman

God, who needs nothing, loves into existence wholly superfluous creatures in order that he may love and perfect them.

C. S. Lewis

Jesus to me is a Shepherd. J. F. Scholfield

The King of love my shepherd is, whose goodness faileth never. I nothing lack if I am his, and he is mine forever.

Sir Henry Williams Baker

Savior, like a shepherd lead us, much we need thy tender care. In Thy pleasant pastures feed us, for our use Thy folds prepare.

Dorothy A. Thrupp

The King Is Coming

Jesus said, "Keep watch, because you do not know on what day your Lord will come."

Matthew 24:42 NIV

The Story Behind What Jesus Said

Jesus spent a lot of time teaching his disciples about the existence of a spiritual kingdom—a kingdom where God would rule his people in righteousness. But they just weren't getting it. They still thought he would overthrow the corrupt Roman government and put an end to their oppression. So when they began to ask questions about the end times, Jesus laid it out for them.

He told them that things would get bad. They would be persecuted and killed for their allegiance to him. There would be false prophets and false messiahs—all claiming to speak for God. He warned them not to be fooled but to watch and pray. When they least expected it, he would return to deliver them.

Reflections on the Words of Jesus

When times are hard, it can be pretty tough to keep your resolve firm and your feet grounded. God knows it's tough, but he expects you, as a person who has chosen to walk in relationship with him, to hang on to your faith.

There will always be those who say, "Wise up. God doesn't care about you. He's never coming back. We've got the real thing over here. It's great—the answer to all your troubles. And best of all, there is no waiting." Don't listen.

No one knows when Jesus will return and establish his kingdom here on earth. What you can know is that Jesus has established his kingdom in your heart, just as he did in the hearts of his disciples. That spiritual kingdom will give you the strength to watch and pray, to discern the true from the false, to follow the plan he has set for your life until he comes to deliver you.

One Final Thought

Jesus will one day establish his physical kingdom here on earth. Until that time, his instruction is to watch, pray, and identify with the spiritual kingdom inside your heart.

Timeless Wisdom for Everyday Living

The King Is Coming

Be up and awake to what God is doing! God is putting the finishing touches on the salvation work he began when we first believed.

Romans 13:12 THE MESSAGE

We are waiting for what he promised—a new heaven and a new earth where goodness lives.

2 Peter 3:13 NCV

Jesus who was taken up from among you to heaven will come as certainly—and mysteriously—as he left.

Acts 1:11 THE MESSAGE

The exact day and hour? No one knows that, not even heaven's angels, not even the Son. Only the Father. So keep a sharp lookout, for you don't know the timetable.

Mark 13:32–33 THE MESSAGE

The Lord himself will come down from heaven with a loud command with the voice of the archangel, and with the trumpet call of God.

1 Thessalonians 4:16 NCV

He is coming with the clouds, and every eye will see him, even those who pierced him.

Revelation 1:7 NIV

Christ hath told us He will come, but not when, that we might never put off our clothes, or put out the candle.
William Gurnall

With my lamp well trimmed and burning, swift to hear and slow to roam, watching for Thy glad returning, to restore me to my home.
J. S. B. Monsell

The fact that Jesus Christ is to come again is not a reason for star-gazing, but for working in the power of the Holy Ghost.
Charles Haddon Spurgeon

Christ deigned that the day of his coming should be hid from us, that being in suspense, we might be as it were upon the watch.
Martin Luther

Jesus, our watch we are keeping, longing for Thee to come. A. B. Simpson

He who loves the coming of the Lord is . . . he who, whether it be far or near, awaits it with sincere faith, steadfast hope, and fervent love.
Saint Augustine of Hippo

The primitive church thought more about the Second Coming of Jesus Christ than about death or about heaven.
Alexander Maclaren

A Sound Mind

Jesus said, "Go home to your family and tell them how much the Lord has done for you, and how he has had mercy on you."

Mark 5:19 NIV

The Story Behind What Jesus Said

Jesus was stepping out of the boat when the man came running toward him. Crazed, arms and legs covered with cuts, clothing in shreds, and screaming, the man was clearly demon possessed. Jesus addressed the demons, insisting that they leave the man and enter a nearby herd of pigs. When the pigs dashed into the lake and drowned themselves, those witnessing the event were terrified and ran into town to report what had happened.

The man, dressed and in his right mind, was later found sitting near Jesus' boat. Angered, perhaps by the loss of their livestock, the people begged Jesus to leave. As Jesus climbed into the boat, the man asked if he could go along.

Reflections on the Words of Jesus

Jesus typically invited people to follow him, but he instructed this man to stay, return to his family, and serve as a witness of God's power. It's not hard to understand why the man would have preferred to sail away with Jesus rather than go home and face those who had been hurt and humiliated by his behavior.

If you have ever messed up or behaved in a shameful way and then turned to God for forgiveness and restoration, you have probably learned what this man learned. Forgiveness happens in an instant. It is God's gift, free and undeserved. But restoration is a different matter. It takes time.

Restoration happens as you face your past and triumph over it step by awkward step. It often requires asking others to forgive you, even though God already has. And it means looking to God daily as you do the hard work of establishing a new way of living.

One Final Thought

Restoration comes when you resist the urge to run away from your past and choose, with God's help, to do the work of setting things right.

Timeless Wisdom for Everyday Living

The God of all grace, who calls you to share his eternal glory in union with Christ, will himself perfect you and give you firmness, strength, and a sure foundation.   1 Peter 5:10 GNT

Restore us, O God; make your face shine upon us, that we may be saved.
Psalm 80:3 NIV

Though you have made me see troubles, many and bitter, you will restore my life again; from the depths of the earth you will again bring me up. You will increase my honor and comfort me once again.
Psalm 71:20–21 NIV

If anyone is in Christ, he is a new creation; the old has gone, the new has come! All this is from God, who reconciled us to himself through Christ and gave us the ministry of reconciliation.
2 Corinthians 5:17–18 NIV

Restore to me again the joy of your salvation, and make me willing to obey you.
Psalm 51:12 NLT

The Lord helps the fallen and lifts up those bent beneath their loads.   Psalm 145:14 NLT

Lord, come as sweet, healing oil into my weary mind, my bruised heart, and my dried-up soul.

Author Unknown

The house of my soul is too small for you to come to it. May it be enlarged by you. It is in ruins—restore it.

Saint Augustine of Hippo

God regenerates us and puts us in contact with all his divine resources, but he cannot make us walk according to his will.

Oswald Chambers

By the reading of Scripture I am so renewed that all nature seems renewed around me and with me.

Thomas Merton

The difference between worldliness and godliness is a renewed mind.

Erwin W. Lutzer

The purpose of Christ's redeeming work was to make it possible for bad men to become good—deeply, radically, and finally.

A. W. Tozer

Reconciliation sounds like a large theological term, but it simply means coming to ourselves and arising and going to our Father.

John Wood Oman

This Very Night

"I tell you the truth," Jesus answered, "this very night, before the rooster crows, you will disown me three times."

Matthew 26:34 NIV

The Story Behind What Jesus Said

It was the last night—the very last one Jesus would spend teaching his disciples, sharing a meal with them, and praying with them. As they walked toward the Mount of Olives and a small garden called Gethsemane, Jesus continued to share with his closest friends what would occur in the next few hours.

But when Jesus told them that the events of the coming night would cause them to scatter and lose heart, Peter was adamant. He'd given up everything to follow Jesus. He wasn't about to fall apart now, no matter how bad things got. Whatever happened, he could handle it—of that he was certain. In his usual outspoken manner, Peter made his argument. But Jesus knew better.

Two betrayals took place on that fateful night. With a telling kiss, Judas turned Jesus over to his captors. Then, seized with remorse and despair, he took his own life.

Peter was indignant about Judas' betrayal, and he never imagined that he would be guilty of doing something so despicable. But he did. The act was the same; only the outcome was different. Judas despaired, but Peter drew courage from the promise of God's love and forgiveness. Judas gave up on himself and God, but Peter reached out to God and was restored.

You may feel that you have betrayed God, that you've turned your back on him. If so, don't let the bitter poison of betrayal destroy your life as Judas did. Instead, follow the example of Peter. God is waiting to forgive you, restore you, and make you the kind of woman he created you to be.

One Final Thought

Betrayal, like most human failings, has the potential to destroy your life. But it loses its power when confronted by the miracle of God's love and forgiveness.

This Very Night

My flesh and my heart may fail, but God is the strength of my heart and my portion forever.

Psalm 73:26 NRSV

You, O Lord, are good and forgiving, abounding in steadfast love to all who call on you.

Psalm 86:5 NRSV

[The LORD says:] "No matter how deep the stain of your sins, I can remove it. I can make you as clean as freshly fallen snow. Even if you are stained as red as crimson, I can make you as white as wool."

Isaiah 1:18 NLT

I [the psalmist] said, "I'll make a clean breast of my failures to God." Suddenly the pressure was gone—my guilt dissolved, my sin disappeared.

Psalm 32:5 THE MESSAGE

I [God] will give you a new heart and put a new spirit in you. I will remove from you your heart of stone and give you a heart of flesh.

Ezekiel 36:26 NIV

Forget the former things; do not dwell on the past. See, I am doing a new thing!   Isaiah 43:18–19 NIV

God's mercy is boundless, free and, through Jesus Christ our Lord, available to us now in our present situation.

A. W. Tozer

Come to God . . . with the weight of low thoughts, failures, neglects, and wandering forgetfulness, and say to Him, "Thou art my refuge."

George Macdonald

There is only one person God cannot forgive—the person who refuses to come to him for forgiveness.

Author Unknown

Do not trust in your own righteousness; do not grieve about a sin that is past and gone.

Saint Anthony of Egypt

I think if God forgives us, we must forgive ourselves. C. S. Lewis

I will love you, O Lord, and thank you, and confess to your name, because you have forgiven me my evil and nefarious deeds.

Saint Augustine of Hippo

Long-suffering, Lord . . . thou delightest to win with love the wandering: thou invitest, by smiles of mercy, not by frowns or terrors, man from Errors.

John Bowring

The Greatest

Jesus said to them, "Whoever welcomes this child in my name, welcomes me; and whoever welcomes me, also welcomes the one who sent me. For the one who is least among you all is the greatest."

Luke 9:48 GNT

The Story Behind What Jesus Said

Everywhere they went, the crowds swarmed around them— pretty heady stuff for Jesus' disciples, none of whom had experienced much in the way of fame and celebrity before they met Jesus. It seems that it was becoming more and more difficult for them to keep their egos in check.

Jesus often made comments in an effort to bring things into perspective, but they didn't understand. Then one day, they began to argue about which one of them would become the greatest. Jesus responded by borrowing a child from the crowd and placing him before them. Then he began to teach them that greatness in God's kingdom is a very different thing than greatness in the world.

Until that day, Jesus' disciples had probably defined greatness in terms of notable accomplishment, fame, riches, and those things that call attention to one's self. Jesus turned the tables on them by teaching that the kingdom standard for greatness is selflessness.

Imagine their surprise when Jesus used a child—someone drawn from the lowest level in the social hierarchy—to drive his point home. Understandably, the disciples' power struggle ended without another word.

Jesus not only taught this definition of greatness, he practiced it by giving his perfect life for the rebellious human beings he had created in his image. This is a principle that touches your life as a woman and as a caregiver on a daily basis. You may think that nobody notices your lowly tasks. But when you provide care for your spouse, children, parents, friends, or co-workers, you are putting yourself on the path to greatness.

One Final Thought

Greatness in the kingdom of God is measured very differently than it is in the eyes of the world. God rewards selflessness rather than the exultation of self.

Timeless Wisdom for Everyday Living

The Greatest

Don't push your way to the front; don't sweet-talk your way to the top. Put yourself aside, and help others get ahead. Don't be obsessed with getting your own advantage.   Philippians 2:3 THE MESSAGE

[God] leads humble people to do what is right, and he teaches them his way.

Psalm 25:9 GOD'S WORD

Whoever humbles himself like this child is the greatest in the kingdom of heaven.

Matthew 18:4 NIV

Remind your people to . . . be obedient, always ready to do what is good. They must not speak evil of anyone, and they must avoid quarreling. Instead, they should be gentle and show true humility to everyone.

Titus 3:1–2 NLT

The brother in humble circumstances ought to take pride in his high position. But the one who is rich should take pride in his low position, because he will pass away like a wild flower.

James 1:9–10 NIV

Humble yourselves before the Lord, and he will lift you up.   James 4:10 NIV

Let the proud seek and love earthly kingdoms, but blessed are the poor in spirit for theirs is the kingdom of heaven.

Saint Augustine of Hippo

Make us worthy, Lord, to serve our fellow men throughout the world who live and die in poverty and hunger.

Mother Teresa

Create in me the desire and will to put the needs of others before my own. I surrender myself and all I possess.

Edith Ventress

I will place no value on anything I have or possess unless it is in relationship to the kingdom of God.

David Livingstone

All greatness grows great by self-abasement, and not by exalting itself. Nestorius

It is not my business to think about myself. My business is to think about God. It is for God to think about me.

Simone Weil

When you become like a child, your pride will melt away and you will be like Christ himself in the stable at Bethlehem.

Martin Luther

107

A House Divided

Jesus said unto them, "Every kingdom divided against itself is brought to desolation; and every city or house divided against itself shall not stand."

Matthew 12:25 KJV

The Story Behind What Jesus Said

Reports that Jesus was performing miracles was drawing large crowds. Families were bringing their sick, deaf, blind, crippled, even demon-possessed loved ones and laying them at Jesus' feet. He restored their bodies and minds, and, in an effort not to incite the Pharisees, he cautioned them to keep quiet about their healing. But the men of the law were not waiting for reports; they were watching, eager to find something they could use to discredit him.

When Jesus healed a demon-possessed man who was also blind and deaf, a buzz went through the crowd. "This must be the Son of God," they whispered. Hearing this, the Pharisees protested, attributing Jesus' miracle-working power to the devil. Their slanderous remarks did not go unchallenged.

Christianity includes a host of denominations, and even inside denominational walls, doctrinal interpretations and differing views proliferate. Some denominations believe in modern-day miracles, while others insist that miracles were reserved for Jesus and the early apostles of the faith. There are disagreements about baptism, modes of worship, and what constitutes moral behavior.

Differences are inevitable, and certainly they were present in the early churches. The problem comes when one group attacks the views of the other groups. The words used by Jesus to confound the Pharisees take on particular relevance. "A house divided against itself shall not stand." That's true of the kingdom of Satan as well as the kingdom of God.

Commit yourself to a spirit of unity. Work to minimize differences and affirm kingdom principles such as love, joy, and peace by reaching out to and humbly serving others.

One Final Thought

God has called you to pursue unity with other believers by avoiding slander and accusation. Fighting against each other weakens the kingdom of God and makes it ineffective.

Timeless Wisdom for Everyday Living

A House Divided

How very good and pleasant it is when kindred live together in unity.

Psalm 133:1 NRSV

Are your hearts tender and sympathetic? Then make me truly happy by agreeing wholeheartedly with each other, loving one another, and working together with one heart and purpose.

Philippians 2:1–2 NLT

The goal is for all of them to become one heart and mind—just as you, Father, are in me [Jesus] and I in you, so they might be one heart and mind with us.

John 17:21 THE MESSAGE

Lead a life worthy of the calling to which you have been called, with all humility and gentleness, with patience, bearing with one another in love, making every effort to maintain the unity of the Spirit in the bond of peace.

Ephesians 4:1–3 NRSV

We who believe are carefully joined together, becoming a holy temple for the Lord.

Ephesians 2:21 NLT

Love is what binds us all together in perfect harmony. Colossians 3:14 NLT

I may worship in a different style, but all we hold dear is God's gift in Christ Jesus, who is our Unity.

Michael J. Davis

If we focus on our differences, our focus is on each other. If we focus with unity, our focus is on God.

Author Unknown

All Christians are called to unity in love and unity in truth.

Author Unknown

Unity makes strength, and since we must be strong, we must also be one.

Grand Duke Friedrich von Baden

We cannot be separated in interest or divided in purpose. We stand together until the end. Woodrow Wilson

Lord, we pray for the unity of your Church. . . . May we remain united to you and to each other, because you are our common source of life.

Saint Cyprian of Carthage

It's hard enough resisting the real enemy. That's a full-time job. If we start fighting other Christians we're fighting two wars—and one of them is suicidal.

John Richard Wimber

For My Sake

Jesus said, "Those who want to save their life will lose it, and those who lose their life for my sake will save it."

Luke 9:24 NRSV

The Story Behind What Jesus Said

Jesus had pulled away from the crowds to pray after a long day of ministering to the sick. Then he called his chosen twelve, who had been praying nearby, and asked them a question: "Who do the crowds say I am?" The disciples answered quickly, "Some say John the Baptist, others say Elijah; and still others, that one of the prophets of long ago has come back to life."

Then Jesus made it personal. "What about you?" he asked. "Who do you say I am?" Peter answered for them all, "The Christ of God." It was the correct answer—technically. But Jesus may well have been probing the expectations beneath the affirmation. Once again he told them what was soon to come.

Reflections on the Words of Jesus

The crowds clamored after Jesus because they expected to see the physical manifestation of his miraculous power. As long as they were seeing the sick made well, the blind given sight, the lame made ambulatory, they were fully committed to following Jesus.

But Jesus knew that the time would soon come when the miracles would give way to the suffering of the cross. The adulation of the crowd would be replaced with cursing and condemnation. He needed to know that his disciples had a realistic expectation of what their faith would cost them.

What are your expectations of the Christian life? Are you looking only for sunny skies and multiplied blessings? If so, your faith will fail at the first sign of trouble. And when you've lost your faith, you've lost everything. Be sure your faith is anchored securely in God. When you're able to give up your life for your faith, you will never lose it.

One Final Thought

The life of faith requires total commitment to the person and integrity of Jesus. Only then will your expectations be realistic and your faith be secure.

Why am I discouraged? Why so sad? I will put my hope in God! I will praise him again—my Savior and my God! Psalm 43:5 NLT

I will find my rest in God alone. He is the One who gives me hope.

Psalm 62:5 NIrV

We were saved with this hope in mind. If we hope for something we already see, it's not really hope. Who hopes for what can be seen? But if we hope for what we don't see, we eagerly wait for it with perseverance.

Romans 8:24–25 GOD'S WORD

Our light and momentary troubles are achieving for us an eternal glory that far outweighs them all. So we fix our eyes not on what is seen, but on what is unseen. For what is seen is temporary, but what is unseen is eternal.

2 Corinthians 4:17–18 NIV

Hope does not disappoint us, because God has poured out his love into our hearts.

Romans 5:5 NIV

Those who hope in me will not be disappointed.

Isaiah 49:23 NIV

Healthy questions keep faith dynamic. Unless we start with doubts we cannot have a deep-rooted faith.

Helen Keller

In ev'ry high and stormy gale, my anchor holds within the vail. On Christ, the solid Rock I stand; All other ground is sinking sand.

Reverend E. Mote

I will not doubt, though sorrows fall like rain. . . . I yet shall see, through my severest losses, the greater gain.

Ella Wheeler Wilcox

To wait the promise of the bow despite the cloud between is Faith—the fervid evidence of loveliness unseen.

John Banister Tabb

Faith is often strengthened right at the place of disappointments. Rodney McBride

I shall walk eager still for what life holds—although it seems the hard road will not end— one never knows the beauty around the bend!

Anna Blake Mezquida

God is the great reality. His resources are available and endless. His promises are real and glorious, beyond our wildest dreams.

John Bertram Phillips

More Than Food

Jesus said, "Therefore I tell you, do not worry about your life, what you will eat or what you will drink, or about your body, what you will wear."

Matthew 6:25 NRSV

The Story Behind What Jesus Said

Thirty years of preparation was coming to fruition in the onset of Jesus' earthly ministry. He had been baptized by John the Baptist, had successfully endured the testing and trial of the devil in the wilderness, and had invited a group of motley fishermen to join him. As they traveled together throughout Galilee, Jesus was quickly gaining a reputation as a miracle worker.

Huge crowds were following him, but Jesus knew that most were more committed to his miracles than to his message. To test their mettle, he climbed up high on a hillside and waited to see who would climb up with him. Then when they were settled, Jesus delivered his opening argument—the definitive description of the kingdom of God.

Reflections on the Words of Jesus

The Sermon on the Mount is perhaps the most remarkable speech ever given. Jesus laid out for his followers the width and breadth of his ministry and the spiritual kingdom he had come to establish on earth.

Jesus described the type of person who would be welcome in God's amazing kingdom—the meek, the righteous, the pure, the merciful, the peacemakers. He then unveiled a new morality based on the internal attitudes of the soul rather than the outward superficialities of prevailing religion.

The core of Jesus' thesis was that living in the kingdom of God meant living in complete dependence on God, inviting him into even the most basic aspects of personal life—what you will wear, what you will eat. No everyday / Sabbath Day ambiguity here. This was a new beginning—the hearts and lives of true believers would become the temple where God dwells.

One Final Thought

God no longer desires to dwell within temples made with stone. He wants to dwell in you—establishing his kingdom in your heart and transforming you from the inside out.

More Than Food

I [Jesus] can guarantee this truth: Whoever doesn't receive the kingdom of God as a little child receives it will never enter it.

Luke 18:17 GOD'S WORD

[God] has enabled you to share in the inheritance of the saints in the light.

Colossians 1:12 NRSV

God's kingdom isn't a matter of what you put in your stomach, for goodness' sake. It's what God does with your life as he sets it right, puts it together, and completes it with joy.

Romans 14:17 THE MESSAGE

Our natural, earthy lives don't in themselves lead us by their very nature into the kingdom of God. Their very "nature" is to die, so how could they "naturally" end up in the Life kingdom?

1 Corinthians 15:50 THE MESSAGE

Seek first [God's] kingdom and his righteousness.

Matthew 6:33 NIV

The kingdom of God is within you.

Luke 17:21 NIV

There can be no kingdom of God in the world without the kingdom of God in our hearts.

Albert Schweitzer

To accept His kingdom and to enter it brings blessedness, because the best conceivable thing is that we should be in obedience to the will of God.

C. H. Dodd

The core of all that Jesus teaches about the kingdom is the immediate apprehension and acceptance of God as King in his own life.

T. W. Mason

Wherever God rules over the human heart as King, there is the kingdom of God established.

Paul Harrison

As the Lord has already told us, God's kingdom is within you. Saint Anthony of Egypt

The indwelling of God is this—to hold God ever in memory, His shrine established within us.

Saint Basil the Great

The kingdom of God is simply God's power enthroned in our hearts. Faith in the kingdom of God is what makes us light of heart.

John Main

Lip Service

Jesus said, "This people
honors me with their lips,
but their hearts are far from
me; in vain do they worship
me, teaching human precepts
as doctrines."
Mark 7:6–7 NRSV

The Story Behind What Jesus Said

The Pharisees and teachers of the law were keeping a close eye
on Jesus and his disciples. They were looking for some reason to
discredit them, and it didn't take long for them to spot a religious
failing. Jesus' disciples were not complying fully with the ritual of
hand-washing before meals.

The Pharisees wasted no time before confronting Jesus. "Why
are your disciples carelessly disobeying the religious laws?" they
asked. "Do they think they're too good to comply with the
simple rule of washing before they eat?" Jesus answered by
reaching back into the depths of the Pharisees' own religious
heritage and quoting the words of Isaiah—words condemning
them for honoring God with their lips while their hearts
remained cold and unfeeling toward him.

JESUS SPEAKS TO WOMEN

The ritual of hand-washing was not part of the Jewish law prescribed by God. It was, in fact, an invention of the religious establishment. It's possible that the Pharisees didn't think Jesus would know the difference. If so, they were woefully mistaken. Jesus turned their condemnation back on their heads by pointing out that the Pharisees were honoring human tradition rather than God's word. Their hands were clean, but their hearts were filthy—corrupt and polluted by sin.

God isn't interested in the illusion of holiness. He never has been. He finds honor in the attitudes of your heart, in the purity of your motives, in the depth of your love and devotion.

When God does ask you to conform your behavior to certain standards, it is in an effort to lift you up rather than pull you down. It is the discipline of a loving father rather than that of a heartless taskmaster.

One Final Thought

It is possible to honor God only when you understand that he is looking for godly behavior inspired by purity of heart and mind.

Timeless Wisdom for Everyday Living

Lip Service

Anyone who sets himself up as "religious" by talking a good game is self-deceived. This kind of religion is hot air and only hot air.

James 1:26 THE MESSAGE

Those who obey God's word really do love him.

1 John 2:5 NLT

The Father . . . has entrusted judgment entirely to the Son so that everyone will honor the Son as they honor the Father. Whoever doesn't honor the Son doesn't honor the Father.

John 5:22–23 GOD'S WORD

It is not those who hear the law who are righteous in God's sight, but it is those who obey the law who will be declared righteous.

Romans 2:13 NIV

Since the Master honors you with a body, honor him with your body!

1 Corinthians 6:14 THE MESSAGE

Blessed rather are those who hear the word of God and obey it.

Luke 11:28 NIV

God is not moved or impressed with our worship until our hearts are moved and impressed by Him.

Kelly Sparks

God has no interest in empty words and gestures. He sees right through them to the heart.

Andrea Garney

Happy the soul which by a sincere self-renunciation, holds itself ceaselessly in the hands of its Creator.

François Fénelon

It is not what a man does that determines whether his work is sacred or secular, it is why he does it.

A. W. Tozer

Worship that pleases God comes from an obedient heart. Author Unknown

You may as well quit reading and hearing the Word of God, and give it to the devil, if you do not desire to live according to it.

Martin Luther

Then are we servants of God, then are we the disciples of Christ, when we do what is commanded us and because it is commanded us.

John Owen

The Righteous Judge

Jesus said, "Will not God grant justice to his chosen ones who cry to him day and night? Will he delay long in helping them? I tell you, he will quickly grant justice to them."

Luke 18:7–8 NRSV

The Story Behind What Jesus Said

The Pharisees, hoping to trick Jesus with his own words, continued to press in, demanding to know when the kingdom he preached about would manifest itself. If he said "now," they would accuse him of treason. If he said "in the future," they would brand him a dreamer. Jesus cut them off with his reply: "The Kingdom of God is already in your midst."

Then, alone with his disciples, Jesus described the suffering that would precede the manifestation of a physical kingdom, and closed with a story about the righteous actions of an unjust judge. "Don't give up. Always pray," he exhorted them. If even an unjust judge does what's right, how much more will your God—the righteous judge—come to rescue you.

The Jewish people were oppressed on all fronts. The Romans had stripped them of their political freedom and imposed a harsh, unmerciful rule. And the Jewish leaders kept them struggling under a harsh burden of religious laws and regulations.

It's no wonder that they longed for a Messiah who would overthrow their oppressors and set them free. They needed and deserved justice, and they believed that they had found their answer in this man of miracles who claimed to be the Son of God. In fact, they had, but it would not be in the manner or the time frame they imagined.

Perhaps you have been looking to God for justice in your life and, because it has not been forthcoming, you wonder if God has abandoned you. Don't give up. Though it may not be in the time or the manner you expect, the day will surely come when God will set things right.

One Final Thought

God describes himself as a "righteous judge." He will bring justice to the earth and to the affairs of your life in his own way in his own time.

The Righteous Judge

Let them praise your great and awesome name. Your name is holy! Mighty king, lover of justice, you have established fairness. You have acted with justice and righteousness.   Psalm 99:3–4 NLT

God will never do anything evil, and the Almighty will never pervert justice.

Job 34:12 GOD'S WORD

[God] won't walk over anyone's feelings, won't push you into a corner. Before you know it, his justice will triumph; the mere sound of his name will signal hope, even among faroff unbelievers.

Matthew 12:20–21 THE MESSAGE

You're suffering now, but justice is on the way. When the Master Jesus appears out of heaven in a blaze of fire with his strong angels, he'll even up the score by settling accounts with those who gave you such a bad time.

2 Thessalonians 1:6 THE MESSAGE

He will judge the world with justice and rule the nations with fairness.

Psalm 9:8 NLT

The Lord is known for his justice.

Psalm 9:16 NLT

God's compassion flows out of his goodness, and goodness without justice is not goodness.

A. W. Tozer

God's justice is a bed where we our anxious hearts may lay and weary with ourselves, may sleep our discontent away.

Frederick Faber

To be perfectly just is an attribute of the divine nature: to be so to the utmost of our abilities is the glory of man.

Joseph Addison

Justice is like the kingdom of God: it is not without us as a fact; it is within us as a great yearning.

George Eliot

Injustice never rules forever.

Lucius Annaeus Seneca

Justice is the firm and continuous desire to render to everyone that which is due.

Justinian

Inasmuch as he is the one true God, wholly incomprehensible and inaccessible to man's understanding, it is reasonable, indeed inevitable, that his justice also should be incomprehensible.

Martin Luther

Watch and Pray

Jesus said, "Keep watch and pray that you will not fall into temptation. The spirit is willing, but the flesh is weak."

Matthew 26:41 GNT

The Story Behind What Jesus Said

It was the end of a long and emotional week for Jesus' disciples. There had been extended ministry to the sick and disadvantaged, and numerous confrontations with the religious leaders. Then they had prepared a Passover meal, during which Jesus spoke of betrayal, heartache, and separation. It's hardly surprising that the men were exhausted by the time they reached the Garden of Gethsemane for a late-night prayer meeting.

Since praying together was such an integral part of their daily routine, the disciples probably never suspected that there in that quiet garden, a battle for the salvation of the world was taking place. As Jesus engaged in a life-and-death struggle—so cataclysmic that it would resound through eternity—his chosen ones nodded off nearby.

Reflections on the Words of Jesus

Jesus' disciples probably knew by now that a major confrontation was coming, but they may have thought Jesus, with God's help, would prevail against their enemies. After all, he was the Messiah. Despite Jesus' many attempts to prepare them, they still had no idea what was really at stake.

There in the Garden of Gethsemane, Jesus was being pressed beyond their comprehension. The humanity of his flesh was battling for its very life as the deity of his spirit determined to carry out the will of the Father. If his flesh prevailed, humankind would be doomed and hopelessly enslaved to sin. If his spirit triumphed, God's blighted creation would be redeemed.

In the end, Jesus' disciples failed to watch and pray. They did not persevere, but Jesus did. He fought the unimaginable battle and won deliverance for those men who slept nearby as well as deliverance for you.

One Final Thought

Jesus persevered against forces far greater than those you will ever encounter. He is calling you to be a woman who also perseveres through prayer and watchfulness.

129

Timeless Wisdom for Everyday Living

Don't throw away your bold faith. It will bring you rich rewards. You need to be faithful. Then you will do what God wants. You will receive what he has promised. Hebrews 10:35–36 NIrV

In his kindness God called you to his eternal glory by means of Jesus Christ. After you have suffered a little while, he will restore, support, and strengthen you, and he will place you on a firm foundation.
1 Peter 5:10 NLT

Perseverance must finish its work so that you may be mature and complete, not lacking anything.
James 1:4 NIV

[God] will give everlasting life to those who search for glory, honor, and immortality by persisting in doing what is good.
Romans 2:7 GOD'S WORD

LORD, you will give perfect peace to anyone who commits himself to be faithful to you. That's because he trusts in you. Trust in the LORD forever. The LORD is the Rock.
Isaiah 26:3–4 NIrV

If we stick it out with him, we'll rule with him.
2 Timothy 2:12 THE MESSAGE

When a train goes through a tunnel and it gets dark, you don't throw away your ticket and jump off. You sit still and trust the engineer.

Corrie ten Boom

There is a strength of quiet endurance as significant of courage as the most daring feats of prowess.

Henry Theodore Tuckerman

Not in the achievement, but in the endurance of the human soul does it show its divine grandeur and its alliance with the infinite God.

Edwin Hubbel Chapin

No one is wise, no one is faithful, no one excels in dignity, but the Christian: and no one is a Christian but he who perseveres even to the end.

Quintus Tertullian

The perseverance of the saints is only possible because of the perseverance of God. J. Oswald Sanders

Permanence, perseverance, and persistence in spite of all obstacles, discouragements, and impossibilities: It is this that in all things distinguishes the strong soul from the weak.

Thomas Carlyle

Perseverance is the sister of patience, the daughter of constancy, the friend of peace, the cementer of friendships, the bond of harmony and the bulwark of holiness.

Saint Bernard of Clairvaux

131

Born Again

Jesus said, "I tell you the truth, no one can see the kingdom of God unless he is born again."

John 3:3 NIV

The Story Behind What Jesus Said

A young man named Nicodemus moved through the shadows, hoping to avoid detection as he made his way to the place where Jesus, a controversial new teacher, was staying. Paying anyone a visit at that hour of the night was awkward, but he had no choice. He had heard Jesus teaching about the kingdom of God and seen the miracles he performed. Now he had questions—questions only Jesus could answer. But Nicodemus was a Pharisee, and he couldn't risk being caught asking them.

Standing before Jesus, Nicodemus began with a declaration: "You are a teacher come from God." And from there, Jesus took the lead. Slowly and carefully, he presented the kingdom of God to Nicodemus—a spiritual kingdom that required a spiritual birth.

Spiritual insight enters first through the heart and then invades the mind like a bright light suddenly expelling the darkness. And revelation is what Nicodemus received as he stood face-to-face with Jesus in the nighttime shadows.

As a Pharisee, Nicodemus had viewed Jesus as a renegade—an arrogant troublemaker who flouted their strict religious traditions. But as he and the members of his sect followed Jesus, watching for a chance to publicly denounce him, Nicodemus watched with an open heart. When he saw bodies being healed and lives being transformed, questions were raised in his mind, questions that his heart answered instantly when he looked into Jesus' eyes.

Have you been considering the claims of Christ only with your mind? If so, it's time to open your heart. Jesus is waiting to reveal himself to you, just as he did to Nicodemus.

One Final Thought

Revelation is more than mental gymnastics; it is the soul's response to truth. Only by revelation can a woman know with certainty that Jesus is the Son of God.

Timeless Wisdom for Everyday Living

Born Again

Jesus said, "No one knows who the Son is except the Father, and who the Father is except the Son, and the one to whom the Son wills to reveal Him." Luke 10:22 NKJV

My eyes will be watching the faithful people in the land so that they may live with me.

Psalm 101:6 GOD'S WORD

The gospel that was proclaimed by me [Paul] is not of human origin; for I did not receive it from a human source, nor was I taught it, but I received it through a revelation of Jesus Christ.

Galatians 1:11–12 NRSV

That the God of our Lord Jesus Christ, the Father of glory, may give to you the spirit of wisdom and revelation in the knowledge of Him, the eyes of your understanding being enlightened.

Ephesians 1:17–18 NKJV

[Christ] was destined before the foundation of the world, but was revealed at the end of the ages for your sake.

1 Peter 1:20 NRSV

The glory of the Lord shall be revealed, and all people shall see it together. Isaiah 40:5 NRSV

The simplicity and delicacy of Christ's revelation of God are the surest proofs of his deity.

Walter H. Smith

The core of Christian revelation is that Jesus Christ is the sole legitimate Lord of all human lives.

Henrik Kraemer

As prayer is the voice of man to God, so revelation is the voice of God to man.

John Henry Newman

Human salvation demands the divine disclosure of truths surpassing reason.

Saint Thomas Aquinas

'Tis revelation satisfies all doubts.

William Cowper

Revelation consists of the initiative of God, who personally came to meet man, in order to open with him a dialogue of salvation.

Pope John Paul II

God hides nothing. His very work from the beginning is revelation—a casting aside of veil after veil, a showing unto men of truth after truth.

George Macdonald

Don't Be Fooled

Jesus said, "Watch out, and don't let anyone fool you. Many men, claiming to speak for me, will come and say, 'I am he!' and they will fool many people."

Mark 13:5–6 GNT

The Story Behind What Jesus Said

Time was running out—little wonder that Jesus was stealing away from the crowds as often as he could to spend time alone with his closest disciples. He still had so much to tell them as he sat with Peter, James, John, and Andrew on a grassy knoll overlooking the temple buildings.

As they listened intently, Jesus told them how they would be able to recognize the end times, and how they could best protect themselves as nation clashed with nation and natural disasters rocked the earth. "It will feel like the whole planet is giving birth," he told them. "Many people will panic and believe anyone who offers to save them," he said. "As for you, don't be fooled."

In the face of the terrible hardships that were coming, Jesus was counting on his small band of disciples to remember him—his voice, his message, his presence. They would be able to see through imposters because they had spent time with the authentic Savior. For now his words afforded comfort, but the day would soon come when they would be the very essence of life, a breath of hope in an evil and chaotic world.

It isn't possible for you to sit on the hillside with Jesus, or hear the witness of Jesus' chosen disciples. But you can get to know him through the Bible, prayer, and the enlightenment of the Holy Spirit, whom he sent to lead you to him.

Don't be deceived. Only Jesus is the way. Get to know him so that you can stand strong and true as a woman of God when the storms of life wash over you.

One Final Thought

Jesus is the one and only Savior of the world, though others may loudly state their claim. The best way to avoid deception is to get to know Jesus personally.

Timeless Wisdom for Everyday Living

Don't Be Fooled

Jesus said to [Thomas], "I am the way, and the truth, and the life. No one comes to the Father except through me. If you know me, you will know my Father also." John 14:6–7 NRSV

Many deceivers have gone out into the world. . . . Be on your guard.

2 John 1:7–8 NRSV

Beware lest anyone cheat you through philosophy and empty deceit, according to the tradition of men, according to the basic principles of the world, and not according to Christ.

Colossians 2:8 NKJV

You know as well as I that the day of the Master's coming can't be posted on our calendars. . . . Let's not sleepwalk through life like those others. Let's keep our eyes open and be smart.

1 Thessalonians 5:2, 6 THE MESSAGE

The wise in heart are called discerning.

Proverbs 16:21 NIV

Let no one deceive you in any way.

2 Thessalonians 2:3 NRSV

Take hold of Jesus as a man and you will discover that he is God.

Martin Luther

Christian truth, then, is redemptive truth because it requires not simply knowledge about something, but knowledge of someone. It is personal.

Harold Cooke Phillips

Christ's words are of permanent value because of His person; they endure because He endures.

W. H. Griffith Thomas

I hold the precepts of Jesus as delivered by Himself, to be the most pure, benevolent and sublime which have ever been preached to man.

Thomas Jefferson

Christ is a substitute for everything, but nothing is a substitute for Christ.

H. A. Ironside

Jesus differs from all other teachers; they reach the ear, but he instructs the heart; they deal with the outward letter, but he imparts an inward taste for the truth.

Charles Spurgeon

There are as many paths to Christ as there are feet to tread them, but there is only one way to God.

Lindsay Glegg

139

One Flesh

Jesus said, "A man will leave his father and mother and be united to his wife, and the two will become one flesh. So they are no longer two, but one."

Mark 10:7–8 NIV

The Story Behind What Jesus Said

The Pharisees were sure they could find a way to trap Jesus with his own words and discredit him before the crowds. After all, he was just a simple carpenter's son. How hard could it possibly be? But so far, every question they had posed to him was answered in a way that allowed him to slip from their grasp. This time they were sure they had him. If Moses allowed divorce, how could he say differently?

Once again, the Pharisees were in for a surprise. Jesus did not condemn divorce. Instead he honored marriage, setting a new standard for love, commitment, and mutual respect, and returning the debate to the court of the creator of marriage—God.

Marriage in Jesus' day was an uneven proposition. Men considered it to be little more than a simple social contract that could be abandoned at the slightest provocation. If a man's wife burned his breakfast, over-salted his food, or offended him in any small way, he could send her packing, shamed and with no means of support.

Jesus' remarkably brief discourse elevated women to a place of equal partnership in the marriage agreement—an unthinkable redistribution of social power—and closed by citing the ultimate authority, "What God has joined together, let man not separate."

Marriage today is different from what it was in Jesus' time. If you are married or thinking of entering into marriage, his divine definition of marriage is one that you should seek to establish in your own life. As a woman, God has granted you equal rights and equal responsibility for honoring the vows made before him.

One Final Thought

Marriage is a divine contract between two equals— a man and a woman—and God, who created the institution of marriage and endowed it with honor and authority.

One Flesh

Let each one of you in particular so love his own wife as himself, and let the wife see that she respects her husband.   Ephesians 5:33 NKJV

Be good wives to your husbands, responsive to their needs. There are husbands who, indifferent as they are to any words about God, will be captivated by your life of holy beauty.

1 Peter 3:1–2 THE MESSAGE

A man leaves his father and his mother and clings to his wife, and they become one flesh.

Genesis 2:24 NRSV

Be agreeable, be sympathetic, be loving, be compassionate, be humble. . . . No sharp-tongued sarcasm. Instead, bless—that's your job, to bless. You'll be a blessing and also get a blessing.

1 Peter 3:8–9 THE MESSAGE

Marriage is honorable in every way, so husbands and wives should be faithful to each other.

Hebrews 13:4 GOD'S WORD

Submitting to one another in the fear of God.

Ephesians 5:21 NKJV

Marriage is not a metaphysical status that cannot be destroyed; it is rather a moral commitment that should be honored.

David Atkinson

God is the witness to every marriage ceremony, and will be the witness to every violation of its vows.

Thomas V. Moore

God has set the type of marriage everywhere throughout the creation. Every creature seeks its perfection in another. The very heavens and earth picture it to us.

Martin Luther

As God by creation made two of one, so again by marriage He made one of two.

Thomas Adams

A successful marriage demands a divorce; a divorce from your own self-love. Paul Frost

One plus one equals one may not be an accurate mathematical concept, but it is an accurate description of God's intention for the marriage relationship.

Wayne Mack

Marriage was ordained for a remedy and to increase the world and for the man to help the woman and the woman the man, with all love and kindness.

William Tyndale

Not As the World Gives

Jesus said, "Peace I leave with you; my peace I give to you. I do not give to you as the world gives. Do not let your hearts be troubled, and do not let them be afraid."

John 14:27 NRSV

The Story Behind What Jesus Said

Jesus and eleven of his twelve chosen disciples sat around a table in a borrowed upstairs room, where they had just shared a traditional Passover dinner. Only Judas was missing. The others presumed that he had gone to pay their host for the meal, but Jesus knew the truth—Judas was following through on his mission of betrayal.

John rested his head on Jesus' shoulder in a tender show of affection as Jesus spoke words of comfort to his small band of followers. Before the morning light, he knew they would be facing their darkest hour—conflict, betrayal, and the torturous death of their beloved Master. Deeply troubled and afraid, they would need a supernatural peace that only he could give them.

Reflections on the Words of Jesus

Jesus knew that his disciples were about to lose all sense of earthly security. They had left behind their families, their professions, all vestiges of their lives, and placed their hopes and dreams in him and his ministry. Now they would also lose the comfort and peace that they drew from his physical presence. Jesus realized that they would flounder without the Holy Spirit, who would come in his place and bring them his peace once he was gone.

God's wonderful peace transcends worldly comforts and penetrates the darkest tribulation—even yours. You may think you've got your bases well covered. But regardless of how well you plan, your security can all come apart in a matter of minutes and hours—just as it did for Jesus' disciples.

Be a woman who lives in peace—a peace that will sustain you until the day when you find yourself secure and calm in God's presence.

One Final Thought

Trouble is no respecter of persons. When the dark clouds appear, you will need a divine peace, a supernatural peace that only God can give you.

I will hear what God the LORD will speak, for He will speak peace to His people and to His saints. Psalm 85:8 NKJV

If the Holy Spirit controls your mind, there is life and peace.

Romans 8:6 NLT

There is lasting peace for those who love your teachings. Nothing can make those people stumble. I have waited with hope for you to save me, O LORD. I have carried out your commandments.

Psalm 119:165–166 GOD'S WORD

Do not worry about anything, but in everything by prayer and supplication with thanksgiving let your requests be made known to God. And the peace of God, which surpasses all understanding, will guard your hearts and your minds in Christ Jesus.

Philippians 4:6–7 NRSV

You will keep in perfect peace all who trust in you, whose thoughts are fixed on you!

Isaiah 26:3 NLT

The mind controlled by the Spirit is life and peace. Romans 8:6 NIV

When Christ came into the world, peace was sung; and when he went out of the world, peace was bequested.

Francis Bacon

The peace which believers enjoy is a participation of the peace that their glorious Lord and Master himself enjoys.

Jonathan Edwards

Do I believe in the circumstances that are apt to bother me just now, that Jesus Christ is not perplexed at all? If I do, his peace is mine.

Oswald Chambers

Christ alone can bring lasting peace—peace with God— peace among men and nations—and peace within our hearts.

Billy Graham

If the basis of peace is God, the secret of peace is trust. J. N. Figgis

In a world filled with causes for worry and anxiety, we need something tougher than "positive thinking." We need the peace of God standing guard over our hearts and minds.

Jerry W. McCant

Finding God you have no need to seek peace, for he himself is your peace.

Frances J. Roberts

147

A Place for You

Jesus said, "In My Father's house are many mansions; if it were not so, I would have told you. I go to prepare a place for you."
John 14:2 NKJV

The Story Behind What Jesus Said

Jesus sat around the table with eleven of his disciples. Having just finished their Passover meal, they were, for the moment, relaxed, enjoying a few intimate moments with their Master. Jesus' tone, often intense and confrontational, was now soft and tender, his words warm and comforting.

The disciples listened intently as Jesus urged them to trust him, to trust God. He would go on ahead to his Father's house. "It's a big place—plenty of rooms for all of you," he assured them. Once there, he would personally oversee preparations for their arrival. Then he would come back for them so that they could all be together, safe and secure in his Father's home.

Reflections on the Words of Jesus

Living as they did on the road, often missing meals as they ministered to the crowds, a quiet dinner together must have seemed wonderful—even with the danger that menaced them just outside the walls of that upper room.

Equally as comforting must have been Jesus' words about a home he was going to prepare for them. In the Hebrew culture, the word for home denoted more than a simple shelter. It also inspired thoughts of love, peace, protection, fellowship, and much more. Jesus' remarks also drew in a familiar custom: The homeowner would arrive first and personally prepare a room for the arrival of each family member. This was undoubtedly the "happily ever after" the disciples had dreamed of.

These comforting words were also intended for you. When the storms are raging in your life, find a quiet place where you can be with your Master. Then reflect on what Jesus is preparing for you.

One Final Thought

You can take comfort in knowing that the day is coming when you will live with Jesus in his heavenly home.

A Place for You

You're blessed when you feel you've lost what is most dear to you. Only then can you be embraced by the One most dear to you.

Matthew 5:4 THE MESSAGE

May your unfailing love be my comfort, according to your promise to your servant.

Psalm 119:76 NIV

Remember what you said to me, your servant—I hang on to these words for dear life! These words hold me up in bad times; yes, your promises rejuvenate me.

Psalm 119:49–50 THE MESSAGE

Praise be to the God and Father of our Lord Jesus Christ, the Father of compassion and the God of all comfort, who comforts us in all our troubles, so that we can comfort those in any trouble with the comfort we ourselves have received from God.

2 Corinthians 1:3–4 NIV

I [God] will turn their mourning into gladness; I will give them comfort and joy instead of sorrow.

Jeremiah 31:13 NIV

You, LORD, have helped me and comforted me.

Psalm 86:17 NKJV

God sometimes snuffs out our brightest candle that we may look up to his eternal stars.

Vance Havner

In Christ the heart of the Father is revealed, and higher comfort there cannot be than to rest in the Father's heart.

Andrew Murray

God is the God of promise. He keeps His word, even when that seems impossible; even when the circumstances seem to point to the opposite.

Colin Urquhart

God's promises are like the star; the darker the night the brighter they shine.

David Nicholas

All human comfort is vain and short.

Thomas à Kempis

It will greatly comfort you if you can see God's hand in both your losses and your crosses.

C. H. Spurgeon

No affliction nor temptation, no guilt nor power of sin, no wounded spirit nor terrified conscience, should induce us to despair of help and comfort from God!

Thomas Scott

All These Things

Jesus said, "Strive first for the kingdom of God and his righteousness, and all these things will be given to you as well."
Matthew 6:33 NRSV

The Story Behind What Jesus Said

It must have been a deeply emotional experience for Jesus as he stood on the Mount of Olives, looking out over a massive crowd that stretched as far as the eye could see—a crowd filled with the sick, blind, deaf, demon-possessed, and crippled. Some were crying out in pain; others argued with unseen tormenters. All were there to take hold of a miracle.

Those anxiously waiting to feel his touch and escape their physical and mental infirmities were probably surprised, even annoyed, when they noticed Jesus looking about for a good spot and then seating himself on the grass-covered hillside. But they soon realized he was speaking to them—his words soft and engaging. Straining to hear, the crowd soon became quiet and still.

Reflections on the Words of Jesus

The Scriptures don't say why Jesus chose to calmly deliver his discourse on the kingdom of God while so many hurting, needy people anxiously waited for his physical touch. But it may well have been a simple matter of heavenly priorities.

Once they were restored physically, the people in the crowd were likely to rush back home—excited and thankful, but still spiritually needy and lacking in understanding. Waiting there for a healing miracle, however, they represented a captive audience poised to hear the words that would lead them to spiritual wholeness.

Have you been waiting anxiously for Jesus to help you with some need in your life? If so, be sure that you are in line with God's priorities. Putting the kingdom of God—the kingdom in which you enter into personal relationship with him—first in your life may be what he is waiting for. When you are spiritually whole, everything else you need will follow.

One Final Thought

God's first priority is for his kingdom to grow and prosper in your life. When you are living in union with him, the other things you need will be provided.

Timeless Wisdom for Everyday Living

All These Things

In the kingdom of God, eating and drinking are not important. The important things are living right with God, peace, and joy in the Holy Spirit.

Romans 14:17 NCV

If anyone would come after me [Jesus], he must deny himself and take up his cross and follow me. For whoever wants to save his life will lose it, but whoever loses his life for me will find it.

Matthew 16:24–25 NIV

First wash the inside of the cup, and then the outside will become clean, too.

Matthew 23:26 NLT

Whoever pursues godliness and unfailing love will find life, godliness, and honor.

Proverbs 21:21 NLT

There's far more here than meets the eye. The things we see now are here today, gone tomorrow. But the things we can't see now will last forever.

2 Corinthians 4:18 THE MESSAGE

Heal me, O Lord, and I shall be healed; save me, and I shall be saved.   Jeremiah 17:14 NRSV

The only significance of life consists in helping to establish the kingdom of God.

Leo Tolstoy

Take glory neither in money, if you have some, nor in influential friends, but in God who gives you everything and above all, wants to give you himself.

Thomas à Kempis

When a person is renewed from day to day by growing in the knowledge of God . . . that person transfers its love from things temporal to things eternal.

Saint Augustine of Hippo

God is unable to grant us our heart's desires till all our desires are reduced to one.

A. W. Tozer

When we are right with God, he gives us our desires and aspirations.

Oswald Chambers

Whenever God rules over the human heart as King, there is the kingdom of God established.

Paul Harrison

There are no cheap, easy miracles. You must want spiritual freedom, not merely for your own sake, but for God's sake as well.

Erwin W. Lutzer

The Servant of All

Jesus said, "Even the Son of Man did not come to be served; he came to serve and to give his life to redeem many people."
Mark 10:45 GNT

The Story Behind What Jesus Said

Jesus and his disciples shuffled along the dusty road to Jerusalem. Once again, Jesus took the opportunity to remind them of what would happen to him there—his betrayal and death. No one spoke for a few minutes, and then James and John asked Jesus for a favor. They wanted to be granted positions of honor in his heavenly kingdom. Soon the other ten caught up and began making their cases for promotion.

Jesus settled them down, scolding them for their lack of under-standing. This was no time to be vying for places at his side. Hadn't he just told them he was headed for anguish and death? Were they ready to serve by making the ultimate sacrifice as he was about to do?

Reflections on the Words of Jesus

Jesus' disciples saw service—tending to the needs of others—as a means to a selfish end, a way to gain status in the kingdom of heaven. And yet their Master was about to endure pain and agony for one reason only—his Father had asked him to. That was the beginning, the middle, and the end of everything he did.

If they truly wanted to follow in his footsteps, Jesus' disciples would have to give all for the same reason—to please God. They would have to see service the way Jesus saw it, as an act of self-less sacrifice.

When you serve those in the world around you—your family, your neighbors, even strangers—are you expecting some payoff in terms of status, good will, a sense of personal satisfaction? Perhaps you should consider being a woman whose good deeds are simply intended to please your heavenly Father. Then you will be serving others as Jesus did.

One Final Thought

Doing good with a selfish outcome in mind is not serving as Jesus served. Pure service involves a selfless, sacrificial motive.

Whenever you're trying to look better than others or get the better of others, things fall apart and everyone ends up at the others' throats.

James 3:16 THE MESSAGE

Serve wholeheartedly, as if you were serving the Lord, not men.

Ephesians 6:7 NIV

The human heart is most deceitful and desperately wicked. Who really knows how bad it is? But I know! I, the LORD, search all hearts and examine secret motives. I give all people their due rewards, according to what their actions deserve.

Jeremiah 17:9–10 NLT

Worship and serve [God] with your whole heart and with a willing mind. For the LORD sees every heart and understands and knows every plan and thought. If you seek him, you will find him.

1 Chronicles 28:9 NLT

If anyone serves, he should do it with the strength God provides.

1 Peter 4:11 NIV

It is the Lord Christ you are serving.

Colossians 3:24 NIV

The average church member would do well to look in his concordance and see how many columns it takes to list all the "serve," "servant," and "service" references.

Vance Havner

In God's family there is to be one great body of people: servants.

Charles Swindoll

Service means the activity of the spiritual life. It is man's spontaneous love offering to God.

Sundar Singh

No one gives at all until he has given all. No one gives anything acceptable to God until he has first given himself in love and sacrifice.

A. W. Tozer

You came here to serve, not to rule.

Thomas à Kempis

Go, labor on, spend and be spent—thy joy to do the Father's will; it is the way the Master west; should not the servant treat it still?

Horatius Bonar

If the mainstream of your service is love of God, no ingratitude, no sin, no devil, no angel, can hinder you from serving your fellowmen.

Oswald Chambers

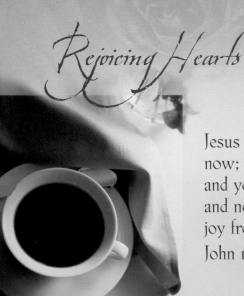

Rejoicing Hearts

Jesus said, "You have pain now; but I will see you again, and your hearts will rejoice, and no one will take your joy from you."

John 16:22 NRSV

The Story Behind What Jesus Said

Jesus and his disciples stayed at the table long after the meal was finished. There in that small upstairs room, Jesus had washed their feet and then talked to them about living and dying. His disciples probably thought of their time together as a strategy session, but Jesus understood that it was good-bye.

There would be no more ministry to the crowds, no more teaching sessions conducted on grassy hillsides, no more sweet fellowship as they walked from town to town. In a few short hours the dark clouds of sorrow would eclipse the sun. But Jesus couldn't bear to leave them without something to hold on to. "This is good-bye," he told them, "but very soon, we will say hello again."

Jesus had spoken to his disciples about his death many times before. But this time he gave them a glimpse of something they could comprehend even less. He was unveiling the outcome of his death—his glorious resurrection. They were soon to face great sorrow, but shortly thereafter, they would be overwhelmed with joy realizing that their Master had conquered death and the grave.

God's resurrection power is at work in your life just as it was in the life of Jesus and his disciples. Yes, there is sorrow—often more than you think you can bear. But with God, sorrow is never the final outcome. At the end of every trial and tribulation, life wins over death and hope wins over despair.

Place yourself in God's hands and allow him to see you through until the sun shines again. It is his promise: Though you are now filled with sorrow, your sadness will soon be turned to joy.

One Final Thought

For those who belong to God, sorrow doesn't last. No matter how difficult the circumstance, how overwhelming the sadness, God will see that joy is the final outcome.

Rejoicing Hearts

You have turned my mourning into dancing; you have taken off my sackcloth and clothed me with joy, so that my soul may praise you and not be silent. Psalm 30:11–12 NRSV

My heart is glad and my tongue rejoices. My body also rests securely because you do not abandon my soul to the grave or allow your holy one to decay. You make the path of life known to me.
Acts 2:26–28 GOD'S WORD

May God, the source of hope, fill you with joy and peace through your faith in him. Then you will overflow with hope by the power of the Holy Spirit.
Romans 15:13 GOD'S WORD

Blessed are you when men hate you, when they exclude you and insult you and reject your name as evil, because of the Son of Man. Rejoice in that day and leap for joy, because great is your reward in heaven.
Luke 6:22–23 NIV

The hope of righteous people leads to joy.
Proverbs 10:28 GOD'S WORD

You will fill me with joy in your presence.
Psalm 16:11 NIV

Life need not be easy to be joyful. Joy is not the absence of trouble but the presence of Christ.

William Van der Hoven

Joy is an unceasing fountain bubbling up in the heart; a secret spring the world can't see and doesn't know anything about.

Dwight Moody

There is a joy which is not given to the ungodly, but to those who love Thee for Thine own sake, who joy Thou Thyself art.

Saint Augustine of Hippo

The surest mark of a Christian is not faith, or even love, but joy.

Samuel Moor Shoemaker

Joy is the most infallible sign of the presence of God. Leon Bloy

Joy is the holy fire that keeps our purpose warm and our intelligence aglow. Resolve to keep happy, and your joy and you shall form an invincible host against difficulty.

Helen Keller

The religion of Christ is the religion of joy. There is every element of joy—deep, ecstatic, satisfying, sanctifying joy—in the gospel of Christ.

Octavius Winslow

163

Filled With God

Jesus said, "Blessed are those who hunger and thirst for righteousness, for they will be filled."
Matthew 5:6 NRSV

The Story Behind What Jesus Said

Every day it was the same—people as far as the eye could see. And among them were some of the most disenfranchised, needy, and hopeless individuals on earth. One wonders what Jesus thought as he looked out over the crowd that had gathered one particular morning near the Mount of Olives. Perhaps he saw not only their broken bodies but also their shipwrecked souls.

Jesus could have done what he had done on other days, walk down into the crowd and lay his hands on the sick and disturbed. See that they had enough to eat. Perform miracles. Instead, he went up on the hillside and began to speak—about true righteousness, the kind that will inherit the kingdom of God.

Reflections on the Words of Jesus

The Sermon on the Mount is considered by many to be a significant milestone in Jesus' ministry. It was as if he drew a line in the sand that day—this is what I am and this is what I am not. It was his business plan and his mission statement rolled into one.

Righteousness played a key role in his remarks on the Mount of Olives. He revolutionized the word completely, giving it meaning it never had before. In his simple and concise style, Jesus rejected the measure for righteousness used by the religious establishment—the unfeeling and literal compliance with every tiny detail of the law—and redefined the term as a hunger and thirst for the things of God.

Are you a woman who pursues the kind of righteousness that Jesus preached? If so, Jesus promised that you will be filled—filled with God and with his true sense of right and wrong.

One Final Thought

True righteousness is more than a strict compliance with the laws of God. It is better defined as a growing relationship with God.

The mouths of the righteous utter wisdom, and their tongues speak justice. The law of their God is in their hearts; their steps do not slip.

Psalm 37:30–31 NRSV

Justice will dwell in the desert and righteousness live in the fertile field. The fruit of righteousness will be peace; the effect of righteousness will be quietness and confidence forever.

Isaiah 32:16–17 NIV

Righteousness from God comes through faith in Jesus Christ to all who believe.

Romans 3:22 NIV

Pursue a righteous life—a life of wonder, faith, love, steadiness, courtesy.

1 Timothy 6:11 THE MESSAGE

Plant the good seeds of righteousness, and you will harvest a crop of my love. Plow up the hard ground of your hearts, for now is the time to seek the LORD that he may come and shower righteousness upon you.

Hosea 10:12 NLT

Whoever pursues righteousness and kindness will find life and honor.   Proverbs 21:21 NRSV

The righteousness of God is not acquired by acts frequently repeated . . . but is imparted by faith.

Martin Luther

The righteousness of Jesus is the righteousness of a Godward relationship of trust, dependence, receptivity.

Michael Ramsey

Righteousness as exemplified by Christ . . . is a consuming passion for God which sends you forth in His name to establish His Kingdom.

Irving Johnson

Any talk about God that fails to take seriously the righteousness of God as revealed in the liberation of the weak and downtrodden is not Christian language.

James Cone

Righteousness is just rightness. Sometimes we make it too theological as a biblical word. Harry Reed

Christ came to reveal what righteousness really is, for nothing will do except righteousness, and no other conception of righteousness will do except Christ's conception of it.

Matthew Arnold

The law as a system was replaced because it was powerless. It could not bring us what we desperately need— righteousness.

Erwin Lutzer

The Greatest Commandment

Jesus said, "The most important [commandment] is this . . . 'Love the Lord your God with all your heart, with all your soul, with all your mind, and with all your strength.'"

Mark 12:29–30 GNT

The Story Behind What Jesus Said

Jesus had no sooner answered the newest trick question posed by the Pharisees and sent them away shaking their heads, than the Sadducees moved toward him, anxious to slay him in their own war of words. They pressured Jesus with a tangled scenario concerning a woman who was married and widowed by each of seven brothers. "Whose wife will she be in heaven?" they asked. Jesus reminded them that the Scriptures say there is no marriage in heaven.

Just then, a man—a teacher of the law—stepped from the shadows. Impressed with Jesus' good answers, he dared to ask a question of his own. It was not a question intended to trap Jesus but rather to satisfy the stirring in his heart.

The first covenant between God and humanity—represented by the Ten Commandments—was a covenant based on rigorous compliance with laws. But Jesus' mission on earth was to establish a new covenant, one that operates by love. The spiritual collision that occurred when Jesus came on the scene was very much that—a war between the advocates of those two covenants.

Jesus states clearly that his intention was not to displace the first covenant, but to fulfill it by changing its focus from legal extremities to heart realities. The teacher who stepped from the shadows was commended by Jesus because he allowed his heart to point him to the new way—the way of love.

God isn't interested in imposing a long list of rules and regulations on you. He wants you to love him with all your heart because you choose to freely give and receive love. Please God by being a woman who is motivated by love.

One Final Thought

Jesus came to establish a new covenant between God and people—a covenant based on love and devotion rather than on rules and regulations.

By coming up with a new plan, a new covenant between God and his people, God put the old plan on the shelf. And there it stays, gathering dust. Hebrews 8:13 THE MESSAGE

The proof that we love God comes when we keep his commandments and they are not at all troublesome.

1 John 5:3 THE MESSAGE

The old plan was only a hint of the good things in the new plan. Since that old "law plan" wasn't complete in itself, it couldn't complete those who followed it.

Hebrews 10:1 THE MESSAGE

Our competence is from God, who has made us competent to be ministers of a new covenant, not of letter but of spirit; for the letter kills, but the Spirit gives life.

2 Corinthians 3:5–6 NRSV

"Because he loves me," says the LORD, "I will rescue him; I will protect him, for he acknowledges my name."

Psalm 91:14 NIV

Jesus has become a surety of a better covenant.

Hebrews 7:22 NKJV

We are never nearer Christ than when we find ourselves lost in a holy amazement at His unspeakable love.

John Owen

The distinguishing mark of a Christian is his confidence in the love of Christ, and the yielding of his affections to Christ in return.

Charles Spurgeon

Charity means nothing else but to love God for himself above all creatures, and to love one's fellowmen for God's sake as one loves oneself.

The Cloud of Knowing

It behooves the lover of Jesus to forsake all other love besides Him, for He will be loved alone, above all others.

Thomas à Kempis

Love unites the soul with God.

Saint John of the Cross

Love is the greatest thing that God can give us; for Himself is love; and it is the greatest thing we can give to God.

Jeremy Taylor

There are many who want me to tell them of secret ways of becoming perfect and I can only tell them that the sole secret is a hearty love of God.

Saint Francis of Sales

Rejoice and Be Glad

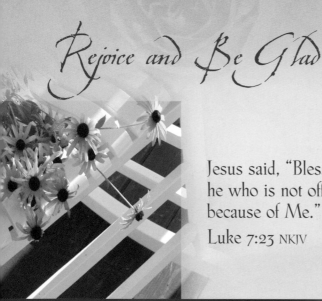

Jesus said, "Blessed is he who is not offended because of Me."

Luke 7:23 NKJV

The Story Behind What Jesus Said

Jesus was beginning to turn heads. One day he had healed the servant of a Roman centurion; the next he raised the only son of a desperate widow from the dead. Many took notice, including some of the followers of John the Baptist.

As Jesus and his disciples walked through the crowd, laying their healing hands on the sick and lame, they were approached by a group of men. "John the Baptist has sent us," they said. "He wants to know if you are the one who God promised would come." At first, Jesus didn't answer. Instead he continued to minister to the people. Then he said quite simply, "Go tell John what you've seen and heard."

John's inquiry was not inspired by a lack of knowing—more probably it was inspired by a sense of desperation. He had been arrested and found himself trapped in a Roman prison. Oh, how the shadows must have played games with his mind. Had he been mistaken? Had he been forgotten?

Jesus' words did not deliver John from prison—in fact, John would soon die at the hands of his captors. Jesus' reply was intended to comfort and assure John in the midst of his persecution. He pointed to the miracles because he knew they would confirm the truth—John had invested his life wisely.

Are you suffering because you have placed your faith in Jesus? Perhaps you wonder if he knows or cares what you are going through. You can be certain that he absolutely and emphatically does. He sees every tear and feels every pain right along with you. Make no mistake about it—you've invested well.

One Final Thought

God won't always rescue you when you suffer persecution as a Christian. But he is always there to comfort and console you in the midst of your tribulations.

Rejoice and Be Glad

God blesses you who are hated and excluded and mocked and cursed because you are identified with me, the Son of Man.   Luke 6:22 NLT

When you do good and suffer, if you take it patiently, this is commendable before God.

1 Peter 2:20 NKJV

God blesses you when you are mocked and persecuted and lied about because you are my followers. Be happy about it! Be very glad! For a great reward awaits you in heaven.

Matthew 5:11–12 NLT

Who will separate us from the love of Christ? Will hardship, or distress, or persecution, or famine, or nakedness, or peril, or sword? . . . No, in all these things we are more than conquerors through him who loved us.

Romans 8:35, 37 NRSV

All who want to live a godly life in Christ Jesus will be persecuted.

2 Timothy 3:12 NRSV

Bless those who persecute you; bless and do not curse.   Romans 12:14 NKJV

Christ's followers cannot expect better treatment in the world than their Master had.

Matthew Henry

Persecution is one of the surest signs of the genuineness of our Christianity.

Benjamin E. Fernando

Persecution for righteousness' sake is what every child of God must expect.

Charles Simeon

Jesus did not come to explain away suffering or remove it. He came to fill it with His presence.

Paul Claudel

The servant of Christ must never be surprised if he has to drink of the same cup with his Lord.   J. C. Ryle

Progress toward the welfare of mankind is made not by the persecutors but by the persecuted.

Leo Tolstoy

Jesus promised his disciples three things—they would be completely fearless, absurdly happy and in constant trouble.

G. K. Chesterton

Receiving the Kingdom

Jesus said, "Do not be afraid, little flock, for your Father has been pleased to give you the kingdom."

Luke 12:32 NIV

The Story Behind What Jesus Said

The crowd was large and pressing in aggressively. Jesus had just harshly rebuked the Pharisees, calling them frauds and pretenders of the worst kind. He needed some time to talk to his disciples about what had happened, but the people weren't cooperating.

Jesus had just warned his disciples not to be consumed by greed and selfishness like the Pharisees when a man pushed to the front and asked him to settle a family dispute over an inheritance. Jesus quickly answered the man with a parable, and then turned back to his disciples. "See what I mean," he told them. "Everyone *wants* something. Don't be so concerned with *getting* that you miss out on the Kingdom of God."

There's nothing new about people pushing themselves to the front, fighting over money and material possessions, using others for their personal gain—in short, there is nothing new about greed. Trouble is, if you let yourself get caught up in looking out for Number One, you can easily miss out on those things that are of real importance.

The Pharisees were so busy protecting their own interests that they failed to recognize the long-awaited Messiah standing right in their midst. The crowds wanted Jesus to heal them, free them, and rule in their favor. But Jesus was determined that his flock—his small group of committed disciples—would not be tripped up by greed.

Jesus' words are relevant for you as well. Don't let greed and self-interest blind you to the eternal riches of the kingdom of God. Let God worry about your needs. It's his good pleasure to give you the whole of his kingdom.

One Final Thought

The pursuit of greed and self-interest will blind you to the treasures God has prepared for those who pursue the interests of his kingdom.

Receiving the Kingdom

Provide yourselves money bags which do not grow old, a treasure in the heavens that does not fail, where no thief approaches nor moth destroys.

Luke 12:33 NKJV

Don't be obsessed with getting more material things. Be relaxed with what you have. Since God assured us, "I'll never let you down, never walk off and leave you."

Hebrews 13:5 THE MESSAGE

Don't let . . . greed even be mentioned among you. This is not appropriate behavior for God's holy people.

Ephesians 5:3 GOD'S WORD

Put to death, therefore, whatever in you is earthly . . . greed (which is idolatry).

Colossians 3:5 NRSV

Do not lay up for yourselves treasures on earth, where moth and rust destroy and where thieves break in and steal; but lay up for yourselves treasures in heaven.

Matthew 6:19–20 NKJV

He who is greedy for gain troubles his own house. Proverbs 15:27 NKJV

Lives based on having are less free than lives based either on doing or on being.

William James

The blessed ones who possess the kingdom are they who have repudiated every external thing and have rooted from their hearts all sense of possessing.

A. W. Tozer

It is so important not to waste what is precious by spending all one's time and emotion on fretting or complaining over what one does not have.

Edith Schaeffer

Theirs is an endless road, a hopeless maze, who seek for goods before they seek for God.

Saint Bernard of Clairvaux

Lord, we don't mind who is second as long as Thou art first. W. E. Stangter

Nobody can fight properly and boldly for the faith if he clings to a fear of being stripped of earthly possessions.

Saint Peter Damian

If we have God in all things while they are ours, we shall have all things in God when they are taken away.

Author Unknown

179

The Cost of Commitment

Jesus said, "This widow has given by far the largest offering today. All these others made offerings that they'll never miss; she gave extravagantly what she couldn't afford—she gave her all!"

Luke 21:3–4 THE MESSAGE

The Story Behind What Jesus Said

Jesus and his disciples watched with interest as a poor widow walked to the front of the Temple to place her gift in the treasury. She seemed undeterred by the fact that her gift, about two pennies, was laughable compared to the lavish beauty of the Temple structure and the substantial amounts the rich were contributing.

Jesus commended the widow for giving everything she had and told his disciples that they, too, would be asked to give all for the kingdom. He warned them that one day the beautiful stone walls of the Temple would be leveled and its treasury plundered. The kingdom of God would also come under attack. His disciples would be persecuted, hated, imprisoned, and even killed for the kingdom's sake.

What was that widow thinking as she placed her last two pennies in the treasury? Did she wonder about what she would eat? Did she stop to consider that her sacrifice would hardly be noticed once added to the sizeable contributions of the rich?

Her thoughts will never be known, but her actions speak of a woman who was 100 percent committed to God. Regardless of her circumstances, she held nothing back. She was willing to trust God completely, giving all she had in exchange for all she needed.

That's what God wants from you too. He wants all of you all the time. Even if it means sacrifice, persecution, and the disapproval of others. Even if it seems like what you're giving can't possibly make a difference. The cost of commitment is high. It requires sacrifice. But the reward—relationship with God—is even higher.

One Final Thought

Giving yourself to God means giving extravagantly and sacrificially. In exchange, you will gain access to all that you need through your faith in him.

Timeless Wisdom for Everyday Living

The Cost of Commitment

Let us continually offer the sacrifice of praise to God, that is, the fruit of our lips, giving thanks to His name.   Hebrews 13:15 NKJV

The eyes of the LORD range throughout the earth to strengthen those whose hearts are fully committed to him.

2 Chronicles 16:9 NIV

I beseech you therefore, brethren, by the mercies of God, that you present your bodies a living sacrifice, holy, acceptable to God, which is your reasonable service.

Romans 12:1 NKJV

Let's keep focused on that goal, those of us who want everything God has for us. If any of you have something else in mind, something less than total commitment, God will clear your blurred vision— you'll see it yet!

Philippians 3:15 THE MESSAGE

Do not forget to do good and to share, for with such sacrifices God is well pleased.

Hebrews 13:16 NKJV

Your hearts must be fully committed to the Lord our God.   1 Kings 8:61 NIV

The principle of sacrifice is that we choose to do or to suffer what apart from our love we should not choose to do or to suffer.

William Temple

If Jesus Christ be God and died for me, then no sacrifice can be too great for me to make for him.

C. T. Studd

All along the Christian course, there must be set-up altars to God on which you sacrifice yourself, or you will never advance a step.

Alexander Maclaren

To sacrifice something is to make it holy by giving it away for love.

Frederick Buechner

If one has not given everything, one has given nothing.   Georges Guynemer

Teach us, good Lord, to serve Thee as Thou deservest. To give and not to count the cost; to fight and not to heed the wounds.

Saint Ignatius of Loyola

There are very few who in their hearts do not believe in God, but . . . they are not ready to promise full allegiance to God alone.

Dwight Moody

What Was Promised

Jesus said, "I am sending upon you what my Father promised; so stay here in the city until you have been clothed with power from on high."

Luke 24:49 NRSV

The Story Behind What Jesus Said

Jesus urged them to touch him, to look him over from head to toe. Some gasped; others wept. The man showed them his hands and feet, ate with them. And yet they still struggled to comprehend the truth, until he began to speak.

That voice—the one that had so often taught them as they gathered on the hillsides and walked along the shores of the Sea of Galilee—was unmistakable. It was the same *powerful* voice that had commanded demons to flee and driven the money-changers from the Temple. It was the same *tender* voice that had comforted their troubled hearts and promised each of them a place in his Father's house. No doubt about it—it was their Master's voice.

Jesus knew his followers would need two things in the desperate days of hardship and persecution that lay ahead—the comfort of his presence and the power of his resurrection. He first confirmed those things through his own Person; then he instructed his followers to wait in the city for the gift of the Holy Spirit, who would be sent to them upon his return to the Father.

The Holy Spirit still abides here in the lives of those who love God. He is the one who provides the power you will need to become a woman of faith. He is the one who will touch your heart with compassion for others, give you the inner assurance and confidence needed to make good choices, and open your understanding to eternal truth.

Jesus, Son of God and Son of Man, will walk on this earth again one day. Until then, he has given you another Comforter, his precious Holy Spirit.

One Final Thought

The Holy Spirit, the third part of God's person, is the power and presence of God here on earth until Jesus returns.

Timeless Wisdom for Everyday Living

What Was Promised

By this you know the Spirit of God: Every spirit that confesses that Jesus Christ has come in the flesh is of God.   1 John 4:2 NKJV

The Friend, the Holy Spirit whom the Father will send at my request, will make everything plain to you.

John 14:26 THE MESSAGE

I [Jesus] will ask the Father and he will give you another Counselor to be with you forever—the Spirit of truth. The world cannot accept him, because it neither sees him nor knows him. But you know him, for he lives with you and will be in you.

John 14:16–17 NIV

The Spirit is God's guarantee that he will give us everything he promised and that he has purchased us to be his own people. This is just one more reason for us to praise our glorious God.

Ephesians 1:14 NLT

I pray that out of his glorious riches he may strengthen you with power through his Spirit in your inner being.

Ephesians 3:16 NIV

The kingdom of God is not eating and drinking, but righteousness and peace and joy in the Holy Spirit.   Romans 14:17 NKJV

God is especially present in the hearts of His people, by His Holy Spirit.

Jeremy Taylor

Jesus promised His followers that "The Strengthener" would be with them forever. This promise is no lullaby for the fainthearted. It is a blood transfusion for courageous living.

E. Paul Hovey

Jesus has gone to prepare a place for us, and the Holy Spirit has been sent to prepare us for that place.

Author Unknown

The Holy Ghost has called me by the Gospel, and illuminated me with His gifts, and sanctified and preserved me in the true faith.

Martin Luther

The gift of the Holy Spirit closes the gap between the life of God and ours.

Austin Farrer

To be controlled by the Spirit means that we are not controlled by what happens on the outside but by what is happening on the inside.

Erwin W. Lutzer

We believe the Holy Spirit lives in us as believers and brings love, joy, peace, patience, kindness, goodness, faithfulness, humility and self-control into our lives.

Toronto Airport Christian Fellowship

In Jesus' Name

Jesus came and said to them,
"All authority in heaven and on
earth has been given to me. . . .
And remember, I am with you
always, to the end of the age."
Matthew 28:18, 20 NRSV

The Story Behind What Jesus Said

The women must have felt unspeakable joy and surprise. They had gone to visit Jesus' tomb, only to find it empty. Then they encountered an angel who announced to them that Jesus had risen from the dead. Before they could get back to tell the other disciples, the Master himself appeared before them. As they held his feet, Jesus instructed the women to pass along a message to his eleven remaining disciples. They were to leave immediately for Galilee, and he would meet them there.

When the eleven arrived, they found Jesus waiting for them. And as they fell to their knees in worship, he commissioned them to be his spokesmen on earth—making disciples, baptizing them, and teaching them about the kingdom of God.

Reflections on the Words of Jesus

Jesus exhibited every strength of a successful, authoritative leader. He led by example and encouraged hands-on experience. He kept his followers focused on the big picture and moving in a forward direction. He loved them deeply, even to the point of giving his life for them.

As a result, his disciples were prepared to carry on the work of his kingdom even after he returned to heaven. They might not have known all they were capable of, but Jesus did. He knew they were ready, and with the help of the Holy Spirit, they would do just fine.

If you are a disciple of Jesus, he desires to invest his authority in you as well. As a true woman of faith, he's counting on you to spread the word of his love to others, extend his hand of hope and encouragement to the depressed and fainting, and carry out the work of his kingdom.

One Final Thought

After Jesus' resurrection, he returned to his Father, but not before passing on his authority to his faithful followers. That authority is available to you as well.

In Jesus' Name

[Jesus Christ] has gone into heaven and is at the right hand of God, angels and authorities and powers having been made subject to Him.

1 Peter 3:22 NKJV

[Jesus] spoke to them again and said, "Peace be with you. As the Father has sent me, so I send you."

John 20:21 NLT

To him who can keep you on your feet, standing tall in his bright presence, fresh and celebrating—to our one God, our only Savior, through Jesus Christ, our Master, be glory, majesty, strength, and rule.

Jude 24–25 THE MESSAGE

The Master Jesus, after briefing them, was taken up to heaven, and he sat down beside God in the place of honor. And the disciples went everywhere preaching, the Master working right with them, validating the Message with indisputable evidence.

Mark 16:19–20 THE MESSAGE

Tell these things to the believers. Encourage and correct them, using your full authority.

Titus 2:15 GOD'S WORD

There is no authority except from God, and the authorities that exist are appointed by God.

Romans 13:1 NKJV

The entrance fee into the kingdom of God is nothing; the annual subscription is all we possess.

Henry Drummond

Christ—in his death, he is a sacrifice satisfying for our sins; in his resurrection, a conqueror; in his ascension, a king; in his intercession a high priest.

Martin Luther

Jesus Christ didn't commit the gospel to an advertising agency; he commissioned disciples.

Joseph Bayly

The Great Commission is far more than evangelism. The Great Commission is to make disciples, "teaching them all I have taught you."

Charles Colson

There can be no kingdom of God in the world without the kingdom of God in our hearts.   Albert Schweitzer

Out of high honor and into shame the Master willingly, gladly came—and now, since He may not suffer anew, as the Father sent Him, so sendeth He you!

Henry Frost

Jesus departed from our sight that he might return to our hearts. He departed, and behold, he is here.

Saint Augustine of Hippo

191